DEATH, HEAVEN, RESURRECTION, AND THE NEW CREATION

KENT BURRESON AND BETH HOELTKE

CONCORDIA PUBLISHING HOUSE • SAINT LOUIS

Concordia
Publishing House

Founded in 1869 as the publishing arm of The Lutheran
Church—Missouri Synod, Concordia Publishing House gives
all glory to God for the blessing of 150 years of opportunities
to provide resources that are faithful to the Holy Scriptures
and the Lutheran Confessions.

Published by Concordia Publishing House
3558 S. Jefferson Avenue, St. Louis, MO 63118-3968
1-800-325-3040 · cph.org

Text © 2019 Kent Burreson and Beth Hoeltke

Unless otherwise indicated, Scripture quotations are from the ESV Bible® (The Holy Bible, English Standard Version®), copyright © 2001 by Crossway, a publishing ministry of Good News Publishers. Used by
permission. All rights reserved.

Hymn texts with the abbreviation *LSB* are from *Lutheran Service Book*, copyright © 2006 Concordia
Publishing House. All rights reserved.

Excerpt from THE JERUSALEM BIBLE copyright © 1966 by Darton, Longman & Todd, Ltd., and
Doubleday, a division of Penguin Random House, LLC. Reprinted by permission.

Excerpt from *Mourning into Dancing* copyright © 1992 by Walter Wangerin Jr. Used by permission of
Zondervan, www.zondervan.com.

THE GREAT DIVORCE by C. S. Lewis copyright © C. S. Lewis Pte. Ltd. 1946. Extract reprinted by
permission.

Manufactured in the United States of America

1 2 3 4 5 6 7 8 9 10   28 27 26 25 24 23 22 21 20 19

PREFACE 6

CHAPTER 1: THE GIFT OF THE BODY

Introduction 7

The Created Body 7

    The Personal Body within the Corporate Body of Persons 7

    The Body as the Whole Person—Body and Spirit 11

    The Body as a Dimension of Our Person 12

    The Body in the Image and Likeness of God 14

    The Fallen Body 17

    The Flesh and the Body in Relation to Sin 18

    The Corporate Body of Persons in Relation to Sin 20

The Crucified and Resurrected Body of Christ: One New Man 22

Christ Jesus, Son of God: Restorer of Humanity 22

    Restorer of Humanity through His Story 25

    Restorer of Humanity through His Incarnation 25

    Restorer of Humanity through His Baptism 26

    Restorer of Humanity through His Transfiguration 27

    Restorer of Humanity through His Supper 28

    Restorer of Humanity through His Death and Resurrection 30

    Restorer of Humanity through His Ascension 32

    Restorer of Humanity through His Coming 32

Preparing the Body for Death and Resurrection: 34
The Potter Molding the Clay

Preparing for Death and Resurrection: Our Baptismal Body 36

Preparing for Death and Resurrection: Our Corporate, 38
Eucharistic Body

Conclusion 39

CHAPTER 2: YOUR DEATH, YOUR DYING

Introduction 42

The Act of Dying 44

Opening Discussion about Death 47

Understanding Death: Medically 48

Understanding Death: A Christian Perspective 52

The Soul 55

The Culture's Understanding of the Soul 60

Challenging Texts on the Soul   61
Awaiting Resurrection: The Time between Death and Resurrection   66
Conclusion   74

CHAPTER 3: FACING THE PERSONAL REALITY OF DEATH: FINDING THE "NEW NORMAL"

Introduction   77
Wangerin's Acts of Grief   79
    Act I: Shock   79
    Act II: Wrestling with the Angel   79
    Act III: Sadness Only   80
    Act IV: Resurrection   82
The Death of Our Loved Ones   83
    Death of a Child by Stillbirth or Miscarriage   83
    Death of a Child   86
    From a Sister's Perspective   89
    Death of a Parent   91
    Death of a Spouse   92
    Death by Suicide   94
    Death via a Terminal Disease   96
    Death of a Pet   99
Things *Not* to Say to Someone Who Is Grieving   100
    Loss of a Child through Miscarriage or Stillbirth   100
    For Any Loss   101
Luther's Word of Comfort to Those Who Grieve   102
What Those Who Are Grieving Want You to Know   102
Our Help Comes from the Lord   103

CHAPTER 4: YOUR VICTORY—THE BODY'S RESURRECTION

Introduction   105
Victory over Death: Christ Jesus' Bodily Resurrection   106
The Last Great Enemy: Death   108
The Reality of Death   110
The Cross as the Sign of Victory Over Death   115
The Creator's Final Molding of the Clay—Your Victory
    Over Death in Your Resurrection   120
The Resurrection of the Cosmos   125
Resurrection Hope in Uncertain Situations   130

The Judgment   132

The Place of Eternal Separation: Hell   135

Our Victorious Hope   138

CHAPTER 5: RECASTING HEAVEN: THE NEW CREATION

Introduction   144

Biblical Understanding   146

Heaven as a Metaphor   147

The Bible and Heaven   149

The Church Fathers and Luther on Heaven   151

    Cyprian   152

    Lactantius   152

    Tertullian   153

    Ephraim of Syria   153

    Ambrose of Milan   154

    The Cappadocians   154

    Augustine   154

    Martin Luther   155

Taking Our Eyes Off Christ   156

Understanding Eternity to Understand Heaven   159

Heaven Recast toward the New Creation   161

Conclusion   166

CHAPTER 6: BODILY LIFE IN GOD'S HEAVENLY CREATION

Introduction   169

Living in the Kingdom of God on the New Earth   169

Our Dwelling Place: The Kingdom of God on the New Earth   171

Agents of the Rule and Reign of God   173

Bodily Life in the New Heaven and the New Earth   177

A Spiritual Body   182

Spiritual: God's Life Reflected in Our Bodies   184

Image God on the New Earth   186

Physical: Relating to One Another and the New Earth   187
    through Our Bodies in the New Creation

Conclusion   191

APPENDIX: COMFORTING HYMNS AND CHRISTIAN SONGS   193

PREFACE

This book came about out of the love we have for God's people, the church. From that love we wrote this book so the church might fully know that death never can destroy the core of human life through faith in the incarnate Christ. We hope that this book will serve as a vehicle for the subject of death to be brought into the light of Christian conversation and will promote discussions regarding what it means for a Christian to die in Christ.

Having known each other for years through various facets of our lives, we attended a liturgical conference and, unbeknownst to either of us, registered for a preconference workshop on natural burial practices. We share common interests in liturgical theology and the theology of creation and Christian practices of worship and caring for creation, so considering how Christians should bury their dead in ways faithful to a biblical and creedal confession was a natural path for us to follow together.

This book grew out of that intersection and our ongoing discussion of and advocacy for natural burial. We quickly realized, however, that it is difficult to talk about burial without thinking about death and dying. First, we had to consider how Christians ponder death and encounter the reality of dying in their own lives and in the lives of those surrounding them in the Body of Christ. So, this book facilitates such a discussion of death, placing it in the context of God's creation of the body and God's resurrection of the body in His Son, Jesus Christ.

May this study provide you with a hope-filled foretaste of bodily life after death, eternally in the presence of Christ.

Beth Hoeltke and Kent Burreson
November 16, 2018
Concordia Seminary, St. Louis, Missouri

CHAPTER 1

THE GIFT OF THE BODY

Introduction

You formed my inward parts; You knitted me together
in my mother's womb. I praise You, for I am fearfully
and wonderfully made. Wonderful are Your works; my
soul knows it very well. My frame was not hidden from
You, when I was being made in secret, intricately woven
in the depths of the earth. Your eyes saw my unformed
substance; in Your book were written, every one of them,
the days that were formed for me, when as yet there was
none of them. (Psalm 139:13–16)

The Created Body

THE PERSONAL BODY WITHIN
THE CORPORATE BODY OF PERSONS

If there is at least one thing we can say about our human bodies, it is that
God calls our bodies, along with everything that He created, "very good"
(Genesis 1:27, 31). Since God as the divine artist forms humans from the dust
of the ground and breathes into them the breath of life (Genesis 2:7), our bodies have divine potency and are animated with the very breath/spirit of God
(*ruach*). Our bodies live because of God's creative handiwork and His gift of
life that permeates every cell of our bodies. It is a personal matter with God.
He personally crafts each of us individually, and in that individuality, He calls
forth our name and our identity.

Our bodies are part of what makes us unique individuals. No two people
are completely alike. Take genetically identical twins, for example. (I know;
my wife is one.) While these twins' bodies appear the same, they are still different. There are differences in shape, skin color, hair length, skin markings,

and so forth. Once one gets to know identical twins, they can be differentiated through these bodily differences. The uniqueness of our bodies points toward the beauty of God's craftsmanship and affirms God's judgment that our bodies are good.

In God's good provision, we can't generate our own bodies. Our bodies come from outside of us, from our parents. Through their bodily union, each of us was conceived and born. Our bodily lives are purely a gift from God through our parents. But as many childless couples know, the power to generate bodies for children does not reside in parents either. Abraham and Sarah knew this well, as they lived to an old age without having borne children:

> Abram said, "Behold, You have given me no offspring, and a member of my household will be my heir." And behold, the word of the LORD came to him: "This man shall not be your heir; your very own son shall be your heir." And He brought him outside and said, "Look toward heaven, and number the stars, if you are able to number them." Then He said to him, "So shall your offspring be." And he believed the LORD, and He counted it to him as righteousness. (Genesis 15:3–6)

Abraham and Sarah received their son, Isaac, as a gift from God, and through them Isaac received his body and his life as a gift. When we perceive by His Word that our bodies are a gift God gives, then living in our bodies enables us to physically experience the grace and love of the Creator. It is the first act of God's love to give each of us our unique body: God's gift to be treasured and honored.

Yet, human experience and understanding distort our receiving our bodies as a gift of God. Think about how science and medicine have informed us to think about the body. For scientific and research purposes, the body can be distinguished from other elements of our person such as our mind and our personality. The body is an object for exploration and examination, something to be grasped and comprehended. Of itself, this isn't a bad thing. Science and medicine have made significant advances in knowing how our bodies function, how complex and wondrous they are, and how most effectively to heal them. But with this approach to the body, we modern Westerners tend to treat our bodies as separate and distinct from who we are as persons. They can become merely vessels or containers for the really important things, whatever those might be: our thoughts, our emotions, our desires, our memories. But God's Word treasures the body as a fundamentally constitutive element of our very being, our person.

An old television commercial encouraged consumers not to leave home without their American Express card. Without it, people wouldn't be able to purchase anything, the ad implied. Of course, that's not true. But it is true that you can't leave home without your body. Who you are is always carried within your body. You can't leave home, or do anything, without it.

Just as you can't do anything without your body, you also can't live in your body apart from other human beings. God created you as a being who lives in your body in bodily relationship to others. At the beginning, the Lord God stated that Adam was bereft of a human companion and helper who was a person like him in bodily form. So, He artistically formed Eve from Adam's body, and they became the first human community (Genesis 2:18–25).

As a result, we have been relating to one another through our bodies ever since. Human creatures function as a corporate body of persons relating to one another in diverse bodily ways and with various levels of intimacy. From eye contact to hearing the voice's sound waves, from adopting the same postures at work and at play to making gestures with our bodies and toward others' bodies, from handshakes and hugs to kisses on the cheek, from caring for the bodies of the ill to the physical love expressed between husband and wife, we communicate with one another and share the common task of living as God's creatures in bodily ways. God created us to be creatures who relate to one another in and through our bodies.

We are bound together through our bodies. And we live in the world with our bodies. We interact with all other creatures and the entire inanimate creation through our bodies: seeing grand vistas and roaring waterfalls, swimming in the ocean and touching and walking in the sand on the seashore, feeling the crawl of a caterpillar on one's skin and feeling a giraffe's sandpaper tongue as it takes food from one's hand, digging a hole in the ground to plant a sapling and leaning against the trunk of a 150-year-old tree. None of that is possible apart from our bodies. We live *in* the world and *with* the world as physical creatures.

QUESTIONS FOR DISCUSSION

In what ways does your body reveal your individual identity?

Our bodies are remarkable. They share certain traits and characteristics with others, especially those in our family, yet they are unique. The way we live, our emotions, and how we interact with other people, nature, and our environment all is revealed through our bodies. Our individual identities don't exist apart from our bodies.

What are the implications of treating your body as a vessel for what you really are as a person rather than a central part of what makes you a person?

When we treat the body as just a vessel for the "real me" (spirit, personality), we denigrate the body and are more prone to neglect our physical needs, mistreat our body, and not care for it as God desires. It can compromise our health, devalue the physical ways in which we engage the world around us, and raise obstacles to fully accomplishing God's will in fulfilling the roles He has given us. We can also devalue the sanctity of the body God created when we think that we can use it for whatever purpose we can justify rather than recognizing it as the temple of God.

Beyond what is indicated here, how do we relate to one another as a corporate body of persons, interacting with our bodies? Why is this important in light of our identity as children of the triune God?

Building a society and cultures in which people can live and thrive demands that people work together. Our interactions for the sake of the common good can't take place apart from our engagement with one another in our bodies. We need one another. None of us can exist independently of creation (which provides us with food, clothing, and shelter) and human society. Consider a human society and the different jobs that a variety of people must do for a community to thrive—teachers, farmers, factory workers, service sector workers, law enforcement workers, firemen, sanitation workers, and so forth. This illustrates that God designed us to work together as a human society to serve and help one another: a corporate body of persons.

THE BODY AS THE WHOLE PERSON—BODY AND SPIRIT

God created our first parents, Adam and Eve, in His image and likeness. In these latter days, God has revealed His visible image in the incarnate Word, Christ Jesus. Paul says in 2 Corinthians 4:4, "In their case the god of this world has blinded the minds of the unbelievers, to keep them from seeing the light of the gospel of the glory of Christ, *who is the image of God*" (emphasis added). Christ Jesus is a whole and complete person, His divine nature and human nature composing one person, as Paul says in Colossians 2:6–15. "In Him the whole fullness of deity dwells bodily" (v. 9). So, created in God's image as revealed in Christ Jesus, we are also whole persons whom God joins together in body and spirit.

Our bodies are an integral part of our personhood or creatureliness. It is not that we humans possess bodies as some sort of "add-on" to our central being. Instead, we are bodies. Our bodies are part of who we are.[1] We human creatures are a mind-spirit-body unity. The Old Testament considered the human creature primarily from this unified perspective, grounded in the creation narrative in Genesis 2:7, where God "formed the man of dust from the ground and breathed into his nostrils the breath of life, and the man became a living creature." Human beings did not become spirits with attached bodies, or bodies with spirits implanted in them, but living creatures, spirit and body together, an inseparable union and communion of spirit and body.

While the Hebrew mind primarily thought in terms of the union of the whole creature, the Greeks and Romans made distinctions. The Greek mind considered the human person to be composed of at least two, if not three, parts: body and spirit, and perhaps also soul. Early Church theologians correlated this bipartite or tripartite distinction with the two component elements in God's creation of humanity: the dust of the earth (body) and the breath of life (spirit). A tripartite distinction adds the soul to the mix, often treated as a division of the spirit into two components: the spirit itself and the soul.

The Greeks further divided the soul into two parts: the vital power, which controls the body's functioning, and the animal power, which includes aggression, the emotions, and the desires. Greeks considered the spirit to be a higher power than the soul, encompassing the intellect, reason, and the self-deter-

---

1   This reflects the thoughts of John A. T. Robinson in *The Body: A Study in Pauline Theology* (Philadelphia: Westminster Press, 1952), 14.

mining will.[2] In distinguishing the parts of the human person in this way, the Church Fathers are contending against any form of naturalism that teaches that the human person is just a physical, biological reality: a mass of cells, for example.

The human person is a wonderful communion of body and spirit in the likeness and image of the Word of God, the body and spirit "being distinguished without being separated, united without being confused."[3] It is the union of body and spirit that God created and will redeem on the final day: "Now may the God of peace Himself sanctify you completely, and may your whole spirit and soul and body be kept blameless at the coming of our Lord Jesus Christ" (1 Thessalonians 5:23).

QUESTIONS FOR DISCUSSION

What does it mean for us in Paul's words to be both body and spirit?

Our body's condition affects our spirit, and the state of our spirit greatly affects our physical body.

Describe what it means not to *have* a body, but to *be* a body.

Being a body means that we recognize the great worth of this gift God has given us. Having a body implies that it is expendable and not an integral part of our daily life. This viewpoint makes it much easier for us to misuse, neglect, or abuse our bodies.

If you think of yourself as composed of your body and your spirit, what implications might that have for shaping your life now and preparing for your own death?

This awareness tends to make a person more thoughtful about how he or she cares for his or her body. At the same time, we realize no amount of physical care can prevent our bodies from breaking down as we age.

THE BODY AS A DIMENSION OF OUR PERSON

While our bodies (along with our spirits) make up who we are as persons, we also can view our bodies as dimensions of our persons, distinct elements of ourselves as creatures. Proverbs 16:24 points to this distinction when it says,

---

2   See Jean-Claude Larchet, *Theology of the Body* (Yonkers, NY: St. Vladimir's Seminary Press, 2017), 14–19.

3   Ibid., 18.

"Gracious words are like a honeycomb, sweetness to the spirit and health to the body." Here the body distinctly receives health from gracious words and the spirit receives something different: sweetness. Each receives a benefit according to its own unique nature.

Our bodies are distinct parts of our person. Our person is who we are in our individuality and uniqueness. Each of us has our own unique body and our own unique spirit. Our body and spirit both contribute uniquely to who each of us is as a person. Both body and spirit have their own individual and personal characteristics (see Luke 16:19–31, where bodily characteristics are highlighted during earthly life, and spiritual characteristics are highlighted after death). In that communion within each of us, our bodies take on a spiritual dimension and our spirits take on a physical dimension. They manifest who we are as people by working together. Our bodies have their distinct characteristics in making us who we are, as do our spirits. The world comes to know who we are with the body and spirit operating together.

This is one of the reasons that the modern utilitarian approach to the body is so destructive. This utilitarian approach understands the body to be an objectified entity, not connected to the spirit or even to the person. It is as though our body is simply a vessel for pleasure or pain, useful only for increasing pleasure and decreasing pain. We can see this kind of approach in medical and psychological treatment that isolates the body or the mind/spirit and treats them as separate and disconnected. We also see this in pursuits of sexual pleasure such as pornography, the swinging lifestyle, and sexual fetishes that objectify the body's purpose as purely for pleasure.

Lastly, we see it in the ways in which we deal with bodies after death. The living separate themselves from the dead body of their loved one, consider it simply a shell for the real person's life, and hurry to dispose of their loved one's body as quickly and efficiently as possible. In all these cases the body's distinctiveness has taken on a life of its own, independent of the person to whom the body belongs. This perspective devalues the body and treats it as a dispensable part of the human person.

QUESTIONS FOR DISCUSSION

Can you think of different ways in which you nurture your body and your spirit?

Nurturing your body can include monitoring your exercise, sleep, and diet. It also might include adequate time for sabbath rest, for engaging nature, and for loving physical contact.

How do you treat your body as just a utilitarian vessel?

Whenever you abuse your body, neglect nurturing your body, or simply give no concern for your body, you minimize it as just a vessel.

What is the most important thing Christians can do in response to the utilitarian approach to the body?

We can visualize our body risen, transformed, and glorified in the new man, Christ Jesus. When we see our earthly bodies as God's careful creation, which He will transform and make new and glorious, we see the dignity and worth of the body God has given us.

THE BODY IN THE IMAGE AND LIKENESS OF GOD

No matter whether we consider the body as representing the whole person or as a distinct part of the person, we affirm that God created the body in His image and likeness. Irenaeus, the second-century Church Father, said, "The glory of God is a living human being."[4] It is the total living person that God created in His image and likeness. And the body, as God created it, participates in God's image and likeness. The beauty of God reflects through the human body, which God formed from the dust.

While God did not have a body before the incarnation, His act of creating physical, concrete creatures with physical, earthy bodies shows His desire to relate to us and deal with us through our bodies. And it reveals His love for His earthy creatures that He creates us so that we can physically and tangibly receive His love. In this way God created our bodies in His image and likeness in their ability to receive the tangible love of God. The Father made that completely clear when He sent His Son to take on human flesh and, in so doing, gave the greatest honor and dignity to our bodies. "And the Word became flesh and dwelt among us, and we have seen His glory, glory as of the only Son from the Father, full of grace and truth" (John 1:14).

The triune God created humanity in His image and after His likeness, an image and likeness whose model and perfection God reveals in His incarnate Son (Genesis 1:26). Our growth in the gifts of the Spirit happens in our minds

---

4   *Adversus Haereses (Against Heresies)*, Book 4, 20:7.

and spirits and also in our bodies, in our senses and in the use of our limbs, (see Galatians 5:22–24, for example), as we serve God and our neighbor. Thus, Jean-Claude Larchet writes, "The sense of smell should enable us to detect in every creature the 'good odor of God' (2 Corinthians 2:15); the sense of taste to discern in all food 'how good the Lord is' (Psalm 34:8)."[5] The physical senses grow into spiritual senses, continually perceiving the life of God through all that we experience and sense. For example, we know and experience love, peace, and kindness through embraces, handshakes, pats on the back, receiving blessings on our heads, and so forth. Our bodies, along with our spirits, are continually moving toward the likeness of God in sanctification.

In many ways, our ongoing growth toward the likeness of God is a remembrance of and a return to our bodies as they were created in our ancestors Adam and Eve. God gave them bodies in the Paradise of Eden that were not purely utilitarian but rather turned toward God and attuned to God's will. Adam and Eve rejoiced in their bodies as gifts of God by thanking God and interacting with God through them. The Spirit of God filled their bodies with His purity and life.

In Christ's resurrection is the seed of the restoration of our bodies to the existence they had in Paradise. In Jesus' resurrection we see what the glorification of our bodies will look like, a glorification that will be ours through His resurrection when our bodies are raised from death. Paul indicates this in 1 Corinthians 15:42–45:

> So is it with the resurrection of the dead. What is sown
> is perishable; what is raised is imperishable. It is sown in
> dishonor; it is raised in glory. It is sown in weakness; it
> is raised in power. It is sown a natural body; it is raised
> a spiritual body. If there is a natural body, there is also a
> spiritual body. Thus it is written, "The first man Adam became
> a living being"; the last Adam became a life-giving spirit.

The spiritual body filled with the image of Christ and the light of the Spirit is the end goal of our created bodies. In the rule and reign of God following Judgment Day, our spiritual bodies will never experience illness, suffering, or

---

5   Larchet, *Theology of the Body*, 28.

death. They will be perfectly whole and healthy. Our senses will be fully attuned to God and His will, experiencing all He desires to give us in the eternal feast. So, Christ Jesus "will transform our lowly body to be like His glorious body, by the power that enables Him even to subject all things to Himself" (Philippians 3:21). We long for that spiritual body to be ours eternally.

The body (along with our spirit), created in the image and likeness of God, is what binds us together as human creatures. While we are individuals with unique characteristics and personalities, the human bodies that we all possess bind us together as one human people. Paul uses this common body language to describe the Church as the fulfillment of humanity's common life and identity: "For just as the body is one and has many members, and all the members of the body, though many, are one body, so it is with Christ" (1 Corinthians 12:12).

As we interact with our fellow human creatures, we perceive that existence in the world takes place in and through our bodies as we all live in the body together. There is, mysteriously, one human body that joins us all as creatures. But we only perceive this one common body by faith through the one Body of Christ, to whom we are united through the Word in Baptism and the Lord's Supper. Our individual bodies, personal and unique, point us toward this one corporate body of persons, brought into existence through the Word of the Father.

QUESTIONS FOR DISCUSSION

What do you think Irenaeus means when he says that the glory of God is a living human being?

God's identity is that of Creator and Ruler over all things. His greatest creative act is making His human creature, created in God's image. When fully living as God intended apart from sin, the human creature reflects the very life of God. When we truly live, rescued from the clutches of sin and evil, we can accomplish great and remarkable things that glorify God by serving our fellow human creatures and all that God created.

Can you think of a time when you realized that your senses were growing into spiritual senses, being conformed more to the likeness of Christ Jesus?

Let's take one sense, the sense of touch. Most of the time our sense of touch functions in a very utilitarian way. By it we know that we are holding, connecting, or in the vicinity of something else. We touch things in order to use them. But sometimes touch turns into something more personal. We touch someone we love in order to love them or to receive love in return. Then the sense of touch begins to become spiritual. It is not just utilitarian. It affects our whole being. It may become even more spiritual when we touch something purely out of grace—an impoverished and sick person, someone who has experienced incredible pain, someone who has moved from being our enemy to our friend. Then touch can be a spiritual sense.

In your own words, describe what Paul means in 1 Corinthians 15 regarding the spiritual body.

Our spiritual body will be conformed to Christ's spiritual body. It will be in full communion with God. It will live in the Spirit of God, entirely enthralled with life in God's presence. It will be a body that can be troubled by nothing, for death will be no more.

THE FALLEN BODY

The Word of God uses two words to depict the human creature's physicality: *body* and *flesh*. *Body*, as we have discussed, refers to the whole person, focusing on the physical substance as God's handiwork. *Flesh*, while a synonym for *body*,[6] refers most often to the physical, external, and visible element of our creaturely existence independent of and in contrast to God. It often refers to our creatureliness in its carnal and sinful existence.[7]

---

6   See Romans 8:13, where both "flesh" and "body" are used to refer to the same thing.

7   Flesh is then contrasted with spirit, especially by Paul, as in Romans 8:13: "For if you live according to the flesh you will die, but if by the Spirit you put to death the deeds of the body, you will live." The flesh leads to death, while the Spirit, given to our spirits, grants life (see vv. 15–16). In this case, the flesh (representing the whole person, not just the physical flesh) is sinful, opposed to God and His will, while the spirit (representing the whole person, not just the spirit) repents of sin and receives God's presence and life.

THE FLESH AND THE BODY IN RELATION TO SIN

Usually the flesh represents the fallen body. It is our body personally alienated from the triune God who created it. The body assumes the position of being its own master and so dissolves its relationship with its source, the Creator's Word. The body's independence from the Great Artist who molded it leads the flesh to see its own warped desires as normal and even twists and construes them into being the will of God. Of this rebellious independence of the flesh, Paul writes in Romans 1:24–25:

> Therefore God gave them up in the lusts of their hearts to impurity,
> to the dishonoring of their bodies among themselves, because they
> exchanged the truth about God for a lie and worshiped and served
> the creature rather than the Creator, who is blessed forever! Amen.

When we turn against God and His will, we distort and deform the body's honor and glory. The body becomes grotesque, marred by its rebellion and sin. In response, we seek to cover the marring of sin and to beautify the sinful body. But it is a patchwork job, like plastic surgery that goes awry, always destined to fail.

We gaze upon the sinful flesh's marring of our bodies in their infirmity and mortality. We are powerless to restore our bodies' beauty and honor. In this life they appear incomplete, diseased, and even ugly in their failure to reflect God's grace. Our "flesh reap[s] corruption" (Galatians 6:8). Our bodies are mortal, destined for death. Day by day they are "wasting away" (2 Corinthians 4:16) unto death. From the moment of our birth, our bodies begin dying as our cells start to decay and malfunction. Every day of human life becomes an experience of and a contention with death. Paul cries out for all of us, "Wretched man that I am! Who will deliver me from this body of death?" (Romans 7:24).

Our bodies' ongoing encounter with the marring of sin and the corruption of death creates, as J. A. T. Robinson notes, great tension and ambiguity in human life.[8] As fleshly creatures we are of the earth and live in the physical world God created. Yet, in our bodies we alienate ourselves from God and live as rebellious creatures in a sin-laden creation.

With all human creatures, "we all once lived in the passions of our flesh,

---

8   Robinson, *The Body*, 22.

carrying out the desires of the body and the mind, and were by nature children of wrath, like the rest of mankind" (Ephesians 2:3). We live in our bodies—good creations of God—bound to the world God created. Yet, our flesh whole-heartedly embraces rebellious independence and autonomy against God. It is at best an ambiguous situation and at worst a tense and conflicted one.

The heavenly Father created us to live bodily in the creation. Yet we separate our bodies from our spirits and persons and abuse the very physical creation God made for us to live in and to nurture. God created us to live in the world, but not of the world. Jesus prays to His Father in John's Gospel, "And I am no longer in the world, but they are in the world, and I am coming to You. . . . I do not ask that You take them out of the world, but that You keep them from the evil one. They are not of the world, just as I am not of the world" (John 17:11, 15–16).

A person who lives "of the world" allows his flesh and its desires to captivate and control his life. His body is no longer a gift to be received from God, but a pleasure seeker whose desires must be satiated by the world that is ostensibly under human control. In the very bodies God created, we alienate ourselves from the master artist and from the very creation He made for us.

QUESTIONS FOR DISCUSSION

Do you agree that as a result of the fall, our bodies have become grotesque? Why or why not?

There is no "correct" answer to this question. In one way, our bodies do become grotesque in the sense that they fail to mirror the beauty of God and His Word. They are shriveled versions of what God intended them to be. Yet, in another sense, they are not grotesque; for we continue to look like human creatures, creatures of the earth, whom God proclaimed "very good" on the last day of creation. We are not goblins!

In what ways do you contend with death every day, especially in your body?

Every day some part of you is dying. As you age, this dying becomes more apparent and noticeable. But it's been there since the day you were born. I hadn't had an eye exam in years. I finally realized I should. And when I did, they discovered retinal dystrophy (macular degeneration in those younger than age 55). Who knows how long I'd had it? It's a ticking time bomb. It could seriously affect my eyesight at any time. I am carrying around death in my eyes—and everywhere else.

Describe what Jesus means in John 17:11, 15–16 in your own words.

Though our bodies are continually dying while we are *in* the world, our bodies are not ultimately *of* this dying creation. Our bodies already know the promise that they will be raised imperishable. They are not, in the end, part of this world that is passing away, but they are being transformed through death to be raised as part of the new world that is coming. Until then we live in this dying world, knowing that it points us toward the new heaven and the new earth.

THE CORPORATE BODY OF PERSONS IN RELATION TO SIN

The effects of sin's rebellion don't end with personal alienation. We suffer a corporate alienation as well, as sin divides us bodily from one another. If you have ever visited the United States Holocaust Memorial Museum in Washington DC, then you have experienced this corporate alienation. There one sees the faces and bodies of the people persecuted by Nazi fear, scapegoating, and hatred. The images haunt us; I was especially moved by the picture of the piles of shoes that once belonged to those whose lives and bodies the Nazis destroyed.

Fear and hatred alienate us from our fellow embodied human beings. Yet, even when we repent of that fear and hatred, we still alienate ourselves from them in our unwillingness to acknowledge and honor the pain and suffering they endured in their bodies. We want to keep them and their suffering at a distance by isolating ourselves from their experience. We want to be other than they are, isolating our bodies from their bodily suffering. Corporate alienation is the result.

The corporate body of humanity is divided and conflicted. As a result of our great rebellion, it is no longer one human body. This division manifests itself in the relationships between the sexes, races and ethnicities, parents and children, old and young. These sinful divisions are rooted in our bodies' form and appearance. We pit these bodily distinctions of our ethnicity, race, nationality, sex, age, and vocation against those of our fellow human beings.

Yet, God's vision for the corporate body of humanity that He created is much more vast. In Genesis 15 God promised Abraham that his offspring would be as numerous as the stars in the heavens (v. 5). Israel often lost sight of this vision and restricted the promise to the nation and heirs of Abraham, the Jewish people. An example is the Israelite rejection of the Samaritans, the remnant of the former Northern Kingdom.

But Jesus' ushering in the rule and reign of God through His death and resurrection realizes the expansive promise spoken to Abraham. For the nation to be as numerous as the stars in the heavens, more would be included than just the physical, bodily heirs of Abraham. It would include all those incorporated into the Body of Christ.

Paul says in Galatians 3:27–29: "For as many of you as were baptized into Christ have put on Christ. There is neither Jew nor Greek, there is neither slave nor free, there is no male and female, for you are all one in Christ Jesus. And if you are Christ's, then you are Abraham's offspring, heirs according to promise." There is neither Jew nor Greek. No nationality, no race, no ethnicity, no age, neither sex, is excluded. Christ re-creates and restores the corporate body of humanity. In Him we are fully a corporate body of persons again, as God the Father intended.

QUESTIONS FOR DISCUSSION

How do encounters with the results of the Holocaust or other widespread persecution and genocides affect you?

> One reaction would be repentance, repentance for our complicity in the evil of our own times and lives. It also leads us to long for deliverance from evil and death, including evil that we cannot control. That sense of helplessness and our cry for deliverance, for us and others, lead us to the only one who has buried evil and death: the crucified and risen Jesus.

How do you experience the divisions in human life that are the result of sin? Consider your relationships in the context of gender, race, ethnicity, age, and so forth.

> Reflect on your own station in life, noting how such divisions surface in your family, relationships, congregation, organizations, work, community, state, and nation.

In Galatians 3:27–29, Paul says that we are one in Christ Jesus. Can you identify ways in which our unity in Christ helps us to overcome destructive divisions in human life and in the Church?

The unity we have in Christ drives us, compels us, to seek reconciliation and unity with others, both within the Church and outside of it. We know the unity that Christ creates, a unity of grace, mercy, and love, devoid of hatred, rivalry, deceit, and opposition. We have seen the beauty of such unified relationship and we long to make it penetrate all of our relationships.

The Crucified and Resurrected Body of Christ: One New Man

By sending His Son to take on human flesh and be the peace and mercy of God to humanity through His Son's death and resurrection, God the Father intends to bring to life a reconciled body of His creatures through that "one new man." That one and only new man is the Lord Jesus Christ. This salvific goal is clearly enunciated by Paul in Ephesians 2:13–16:

> But now in Christ Jesus you who once were far off have been brought near by the blood of Christ. For He Himself is our peace, who has made us both one and has broken down in His flesh the dividing wall of hostility by abolishing the law of commandments expressed in ordinances, that He might create in Himself one new man in place of the two, so making peace, and might reconcile us both to God in one body through the cross, thereby killing the hostility.

Christ Jesus, Son of God: Restorer of Humanity

Christ is the peace who has made Jews and Gentiles one in and through His crucified and risen person. His life in His body is the peace of God that restores to humanity its life, its purpose as creatures, and its unity. All this Jesus accomplishes in His person and through His body. Jesus is the restorer of humanity—not only of individual humans but of humanity as the corporate body of human beings, in and through His one body.

God's great endeavor is to make true humans out of His creatures. This great reclamation act culminates in Jesus' restoration of the bodily life of humanity. It can be described in at least the following two ways: Jesus as the Great Physician of our bodily life and Jesus as the Redeemer of our bodily life.

First, consider Jesus as our Great Physician. Throughout the New Testament, but especially in the Gospel of Luke, Jesus is concerned with the emotional, spiritual, intellectual, and physical well-being of His human creatures. With great compassion He feeds the hungry, gives water to the thirsty, heals the sick, gives sight to the blind and hearing to the deaf, and raises the dead. As the Great Physician, He came to cure and give life to the whole person, body and spirit.[9]

As the Great Physician, Christ identifies with our entire body and with the curing of our deadly sin-sickness. He has assumed to Himself all of humanity in His incarnation and crucifixion; therefore, as Jean-Claude Larchet notes, "any evil done to a human being—not just in spirit but in body too—thereby affects Christ Himself, just as any good deed done to a man or woman, whether in body or spirit, is directed through them to Christ" (see Matthew 25:34–45). As our Great Physician He takes into His body our deadly sickness and in Himself heals it to new life.

Jesus is not only the Great Physician of our bodies but also the great Redeemer. Jesus redeems our bodies from their sinful grotesqueness, making them beautiful and honorable in the sight of God and one another. As Paul says in Romans 8:23, "And not only the creation, but we ourselves, who have the firstfruits of the Spirit, groan inwardly as we wait eagerly for adoption as sons, the *redemption* of our *bodies*" (emphasis added). He will redeem our bodies fully and finally on the Last Day when He returns and raises all the dead.

Even now He raises our bodies from their fallen state and reorients them in loving service to His Father's will. He redeems us from the power of death by destroying death through His own death. He redeems us from the power of sin by burying our sin and guilt in His tomb. And He redeems us from the demands and curse of the Law by freeing us in His crucified and risen body from the control of the Law.

---

9   Matthew 10:28; 1 Thessalonians 5:23.

His victory over these forces is a bodily (and spiritual) victory in which we share through our incorporation into His body. As the theologian John Behr notes, "Mortality is not a property of God, creating life is not a property of humans, but Christ has brought both together, conquering death by His death and in this very act conferring life immortal."[10]

QUESTIONS FOR DISCUSSION

Tell about a time when you experienced the "killing of hostility" in Christ of which Paul speaks in Ephesians 2.

> The sad state of affairs is that we are by nature hostile to one another in body and spirit. We have to be told that because we don't believe that is our natural sinful state. Only the renewing Spirit of God in Baptism overcomes that natural hostility, killing it through the drowning of the old human in the cross of Jesus in Baptism. That leads to the killing of hostility in relationship to others. Even in relationships that are hostile or conflicted, the Spirit moves us to see one another as brothers and sisters in Christ through the renewing power of the Word in Baptism. The Holy Spirit desires for brothers and sisters to live in love and at peace with one another.

What is the difference between the healing that the medical community seeks to bring about for us and the healing that Jesus, the Great Physician, brings?

> Jesus gives us His own glorified and resurrected life in His Word, in His baptismal waters, and in the body and blood of His Supper. It is human life that has gone beyond death, conquering all diseases, sicknesses, and physical trials. It is the complete healing and renewal of our bodies in the image of the eternally living one, Jesus.

What is the redemption of our bodies?

> That is the resurrection and transformation of our bodies into the spiritual bodies that Christ will give us when He returns to reign.

---

10   John Behr, *Becoming Human: Meditations on Christian Anthropology in Word and Image* (Yonkers, NY: St. Vladimir's Seminary Press, 2013), 25.

RESTORER OF HUMANITY THROUGH HIS STORY

The Lord Jesus' healing and redemption of our rebellious and fallen bodies takes place through His body in the entire course of His life, ministry, death, resurrection, ascension, and coming to establish His eternal kingdom. Every aspect of our Savior's life is part of the redemption of our bodies, and our bodies participate in every aspect of His redemptive work.

QUESTION FOR DISCUSSION

How would you describe your participation in every aspect of Jesus' redemptive life?

Jesus passed through every phase of human life as our substitute and Savior, so no matter what season of life I may be passing through, Christ is in me, forgiving my sins, and raising me to new life to the glory of God and the benefit of my neighbor.

RESTORER OF HUMANITY THROUGH HIS INCARNATION

Jesus' redemption of our bodies begins with His incarnation, His taking our human body upon Himself as the Logos, the Son of God. As John reveals in His Gospel, "The Word became flesh and dwelt among us, and we have seen His glory, glory as of the only Son from the Father, full of grace and truth. . . . For from His fullness we have all received, grace upon grace" (John 1:14, 16). In Christ's assuming human flesh, the body is returned to honor and glory, filled with the grace of God. In this act God through His Son accords the human bodies of His creatures with eternal value, as they had when God created the human body in His image at creation's beginning. In Jesus' incarnation and birth through the Virgin Mary, the salvation and restoration of our human bodies begins. Through Jesus' incarnation God restored life to humanity and to our bodies.

QUESTION FOR DISCUSSION

What does John mean when he says that from Jesus' fullness, we have all received grace upon grace?

Jesus' fullness is that the Son of God has taken on human flesh and through His life, death, and resurrection has united it to the life of God. Out of that fullness flow streams of living water, streams of grace through His Word, bestowing God's grace, mercy, and love, but also the renewal of our body, mind, and spirit, and eventually, unending bodily life in His eternal kingdom. That is grace upon grace.

RESTORER OF HUMANITY THROUGH HIS BAPTISM

Following His incarnation, Jesus' Baptism in the Jordan River conveyed that His redemptive and healing work concerns the human body. Baptism is an act that engages the body and the human senses. The body actively participates in Baptism. Baptism from the early eras of the Church's life was a full-bodied experience. The one being baptized stood in a substantial body of water—whether in a natural body of water or a font or pool—and the baptizer either doused the one being baptized with the water from head to foot or submersed him or her beneath the water.

In either case, the body experienced a torrential flood, drowning and killing the person's sinful nature. It robustly cleansed the body through the force of the water, washing away the marring, grotesque effects of sin and guilt. One felt the water and heard the water. One went under the darkness of the water and rose out of it again with new breath, light, and life. And the newly baptized experienced all of this with the name of God—Father, Son, and Holy Spirit—resounding in his or her ears, identifying the baptized as a child of God.

It was probably such a full-bodied experience for Jesus in His Baptism, although the Gospel writers don't describe His Baptism with that detail. But they do show that through His Baptism, Jesus identified with our bodies, intending to save and restore them to wholeness of life before God.

At His Baptism, the Son of God pursued His course of life fully in and through His body, and He manifested through His bodily life the redeemed honor and glory of the human person. When God the Father said at Jesus' Baptism, "This is My beloved Son, with whom I am well pleased" (Matthew 3:17), the Father affirmed Jesus' identity as both the Son of God and the human Messiah in terms of His whole person, including His body. In Jesus' Baptism, which we participate in through our own Baptism, God redeems and cleanses our bodies completely.

QUESTION FOR DISCUSSION

What do you see happening whenever you witness a Baptism? What does that lead you to do?

At every Baptism you see God the Father at work in Christ through the pouring out of the Holy Spirit, rebirthing and renewing His creature into a child of God. You see a wonder in the making, in the words of the great hymnwriter Jaroslav Vajda. You see the Spirit putting an old creature to death in Christ's death and a new person arising from the baptismal tomb, the womb of Baptism. It is death-dealing and life-giving. This should lead you to remember and give thanks for your own Baptism, that the very thing being done to this person, body and spirit, has been done to you and that you now live as the Father's child because you are baptized.

RESTORER OF HUMANITY THROUGH HIS TRANSFIGURATION

Baptism points toward the transformation of our bodies through Jesus' death and resurrection. As Paul says in Philippians 3:20–21, "But our citizenship is in heaven, and from it we await a Savior, the Lord Jesus Christ, who will transform our lowly body to be like His glorious body, by the power that enables Him even to subject all things to Himself."

At His transfiguration Jesus revealed the transformation of our bodies that will take place as a result of our resurrection on the Last Day. The vision of what happened to Jesus' body—and of what will happen to our bodies through our incorporation into Jesus—is magnificent: "And after six days Jesus took with Him Peter and James and John, and led them up a high mountain by themselves. And He was transfigured before them, and His clothes became radiant, intensely white, as no one on earth could bleach them" (Mark 9:2–3). As at Jesus' Baptism, the Father's voice came from a cloud, announcing, "This is My beloved Son" (v. 7).

Through Jesus' transfiguration, the Father revealed the personal future of those who listen to Jesus and are brought into His rule and reign. God will give us truly spiritual bodies that radiate the Spirit of God. Our bodies will be filled, enveloped, and permeated by the light and glory of the Word, the Son of God, risen from the dead. We will truly display the image and likeness of God through the light of Christ radiating from our bodies and spirits.

In lives filled with sin and its consequences, bodily suffering, and physical death, the Father grants us this vision of His beloved Son and our future in Him. Bodily life in the rule and reign of God will be beautiful and glorious.

QUESTION FOR DISCUSSION

How is Jesus transfiguring you in body and spirit in your life right now?

Every day of life offers the opportunity for transfiguration. Every day that the Holy Spirit leads us to live in the Word, Jesus Christ, is a day encompassing moments of God's transfiguration. My spirit is being transformed through the joys and sorrows, the triumphs and trials of life, as seen in the story of God's Son, in whom "we live and move and have our being" (Acts 17:28). They offer us glimpses of the refining of our bodies and spirits that God will finish on the day of Christ's return, when our bodies will be healed, transformed, and glorified. Our patience, joy, and confidence in Jesus Christ is a sign of God's transfiguration of us.

RESTORER OF HUMANITY THROUGH HIS SUPPER

On the night that began His Passion—His suffering and death for the life of the world—Jesus offered to His disciples, and to the entire Church who listens to the Word that they proclaimed throughout the world, a participation in this glorious vision of what our bodies will be on that day when He said:

> Take, eat; this is My body, which is given for you. This do in remembrance of Me. . . . Drink of it, all of you; this cup is the new testament in My blood, which is shed for you for the forgiveness of sins. This do, as often as you drink it, in remembrance of Me.[11]

Eating and drinking Jesus' crucified and risen body and blood in the bread and wine of the Lord's Supper is our body and spirit's participation already in the redeemed body that will be ours when Christ comes.

At the end of his remembrance of the Lord's words establishing the meal of His kingdom, Paul confesses, "As often as [we] eat this bread and drink the cup, [we] proclaim the Lord's death until He comes" (1 Corinthians 11:26). When we eat the bread and wine of the Lord's Supper, we participate in Christ's death, which is God's mercy and grace upon sinners.

Yet Christ's death does not stand alone. As often as we eat this bread and drink this cup, we participate in His resurrection, His ascension, His coming, His entire life and ministry. We participate in the rule and reign of God

---

11   *LSB* (St. Louis: Concordia Publishing House, 2006), p. 162. See Matthew 26:26–28; Mark 14:22–24; Luke 22:19–20; 1 Corinthians 11:23–25.

through His Son, Christ Jesus. We participate even now in the Kingdom that is to come. This is the reason Paul asks the Corinthians whether they recognize what they are participating in when taking the Lord's Supper:

> The cup of blessing that we bless, is it not a participation in the blood of Christ? The bread that we break, is it not a participation in the body of Christ? Because there is one bread, we who are many are one body, for we all partake of the one bread. (1 Corinthians 10:16–17)

Participation in the body and blood of Christ in the bread and wine is a participation in the entire person of Christ: His divine and human natures, His body and spirit. So Jesus shares Himself with us—His very identity and His story—and communion with Him in His eternal kingdom.

In communing with Jesus we also commune with His heavenly Father and the Holy Spirit. In some mysterious way we participate in their divine life and relationship. We are creatures brought into their relationship of love and grace, transforming our bodies to be like Jesus' heavenly (spiritual) body.

The dismissal at the Lord's Supper communicates these effects of participating in the bread and cup of Jesus' body and blood: "The body and blood of our Lord Jesus Christ strengthen and preserve you in body and spirit to life everlasting. Depart in peace."[12] The body and blood of Jesus is life-giving! It strengthens and preserves our bodies and spirits, even through our own deaths, to eternal life. As often as we participate in the Lord's Supper, this is the hope that is given to us.

QUESTION FOR DISCUSSION

"The body and blood of Jesus strengthens and preserves our bodies and spirits, even through our own deaths, to eternal life." What does this statement mean for you?

> It is easy to think of Holy Communion as a blessing just for this earthly life—a source of strength and comfort for day-to-day living. But the body and blood of Jesus, which passed through death to life everlasting, is in me to carry me through the rest of this life, my death, and clear through to my resurrection on the day of His return.

---

12   Ibid., p. 164.

RESTORER OF HUMANITY THROUGH HIS DEATH AND RESURRECTION

This hope ultimately is established in Jesus' death and resurrection, as Paul says in 1 Corinthians 11:26. In and through His body, Christ accomplished the redemptive and healing work that restored us to full humanity in our bodies. He suffered and died a horrific death on the cruel instrument of punishment, the cross, and rose with His crucified body transformed and glorified on the third day after His death.

He intends for us to participate in His death and resurrection and in His victory over sin, death, and hell. Thus we, with Him, pass over the physical death that could lead to eternal death and separation from God's presence, and we live and rule with Him in His eternal kingdom. We are freed from the hold of sin, death, and the devil's tyranny in our bodies and from the eternal corruption, suffering, and death of our bodies. Paul describes the impact of Jesus' death and resurrection in this way:

> For in Him the whole fullness of deity dwells bodily, and you have been filled in Him, who is the head of all rule and authority. In Him also you were circumcised with a circumcision made without hands, by putting off the body of the flesh, by the circumcision of Christ, having been buried with Him in baptism, in which you were also raised with Him through faith in the powerful working of God, who raised Him from the dead. And you, who were dead in your trespasses and the uncircumcision of your flesh, God made alive together with Him, having forgiven us all our trespasses, by canceling the record of debt that stood against us with its legal demands. This He set aside, nailing it to the cross. He disarmed the rulers and authorities and put them to open shame, by triumphing over them in Him. (Colossians 2:9–15)

Paul uses the experience of circumcision, a very physical experience, to communicate that bodily we experience a spiritual circumcision through Christ's death and resurrection in Baptism. What was sinful and dead in us God circumcises when He nails it to Jesus' cross and makes us alive in Christ who was raised from the dead. As a result, we live, even in our bodies that are decaying, a new, holy, and righteous life through Jesus. As Peter says in 1 Peter 2:24,

"He Himself bore our sins in His body on the tree, that we might die to sin and live to righteousness. By His wounds you have been healed." In Christ's dead body God kills our sins and sinful humanity, and so we live a new life in our bodies in Christ's righteous life.

Christ's righteous postresurrection life includes His transfigured body. Jesus attains in His body a spiritual mode of living. While it is Jesus' body, it is so transformed that at first the disciples don't recognize Him (John 21:4; Luke 24:16, 37). His body is no longer bound to natural, physical laws (John 20:19, 26; Luke 24:31). Yet, it is still the body of the crucified Jesus, as He makes clear when He asks Thomas to put his hand into His side (John 20:27).

Jesus' glorified and spiritual body is a vision of the body that will be ours when God raises us and we live by the life of the risen Jesus and in the power of His Spirit. As Paul says in 1 Corinthians 15:44, 49: "It is sown a natural body; it is raised a spiritual body. . . . Just as we have borne the image of the man of dust, we shall also bear the image of the man of heaven." This is the vision of our resurrected bodies that God has implanted in our heart's eye.

QUESTIONS FOR DISCUSSION

How is God's spiritual circumcision of you in Jesus' death at work in your body?

God is cutting away my old sinful attitudes and desires, teaching me the vanity of sinful lusts and pursuits, and nurturing in me the fruit of the Spirit (Galatians 5:22). I am learning to control my body, love others in bodily ways that respect the other person's body, use my body to relate to others in gentleness, and so forth.

If you had been one of the disciples in the Upper Room when Jesus appeared to them (John 20), how do you think you might have responded to seeing Jesus' resurrected body?

Perhaps I would have reacted as they did—first with shock and amazement, then with fear. After all, they had abandoned Him, and now He has come back as He promised, and so they presumed that He would judge them. Then, imagine the joy as He announces not His judgment but peace. In any case, seeing a spiritual body would no doubt be a complete and utter surprise, beyond imagination.

RESTORER OF HUMANITY THROUGH HIS ASCENSION

When Jesus ascended into heaven forty days after His resurrection (Luke 24:50–52; Acts 1:6–11), He permanently established the hope for our bodily participation in the rule and reign of God. When He ascended, He did so in His human body, taking it into heaven with Him. The possibility for our bodily participation in His Father's eternal kingdom was established, because Jesus always will live in His body in His Father's kingdom.

Christ Jesus through His ascension raises our entire nature and humanity, our bodies and spirits, into the kingdom of the Father, Son, and Holy Spirit. There we share bodily in the life of the triune God through our incorporation into the body of Christ. In Christ's ascension we see by faith the hope of our eternal destiny.

QUESTION FOR DISCUSSION

Describe how you feel about the hope for your body that Jesus' ascension gives you.

Jesus' ascension demonstrated the completion of His saving work to restore creation. That means it is accomplished—my body will rise from its resting place on the Last Day. Jesus' ascension therefore gives me confidence that He will transform my body and raise it with Him to live in His rule and reign.

RESTORER OF HUMANITY THROUGH HIS COMING

Coming! Our eternal destiny is approaching with the coming of our Lord Jesus Christ. Christ Jesus is always the Coming One, the Expected One, the one who is coming. We live always in the hope of His coming. It is at His coming that God will give our bodies (and spirits) their eternal composition: glorified, spiritual bodies as conformed by the Spirit to the body of the Savior, Jesus.

Paul concludes his First Epistle to the Thessalonians by saying, "Now may the God of peace Himself sanctify you completely, and may your whole spirit and soul and body be kept blameless at the coming of our Lord Jesus Christ" (5:23). Paul prays that our entire person, including our body, may be kept blameless until the coming of the Lord. Elsewhere in the same epistle he expresses the hope for their persons, clearly including their bodies: "For what is our hope or joy or crown of boasting before our Lord Jesus at His coming? Is it not you?" (2:19; see also 3:13).

Yet, the most complete and compelling vision of the state of our persons and bodies at the coming of the Lord Jesus is in Paul's First Letter to the Corinthians. Here he confesses this vision in the Coming One:

> But someone will ask, "How are the dead raised? With what kind of body do they come?" . . . There are heavenly bodies and earthly bodies, but the glory of the heavenly is of one kind, and the glory of the earthly is of another. . . . So is it with the resurrection of the dead. What is sown is perishable; what is raised is imperishable. It is sown in dishonor; it is raised in glory. It is sown in weakness; it is raised in power. It is sown a natural body; it is raised a spiritual body. If there is a natural body, there is also a spiritual body. Thus it is written, "The first man Adam became a living being"; the last Adam became a life-giving spirit. But it is not the spiritual that is first but the natural, and then the spiritual. The first man was from the earth, a man of dust; the second man is from heaven. As was the man of dust, so also are those who are of the dust, and as is the man of heaven, so also are those who are of heaven. Just as we have borne the image of the man of dust, we shall also bear the image of the man of heaven. I tell you this, brothers: flesh and blood cannot inherit the kingdom of God, nor does the perishable inherit the imperishable. Behold! I tell you a mystery. We shall not all sleep, but we shall all be changed, in a moment, in the twinkling of an eye, at the last trumpet. For the trumpet will sound, and the dead will be raised imperishable, and we shall be changed. For this perishable body must put on the imperishable, and this mortal body must put on immortality. (1 Corinthians 15:35, 40, 42–53)

At our resurrection God will change our bodies so that they become spiritual bodies like Christ Jesus, the man from heaven: imperishable, glorified, raised in power. This is the destiny within God's kingdom of those bodies God first created in His image and likeness: human beings who truly live, bearing the image of the man of heaven!

QUESTION FOR DISCUSSION

Put into your own words the implications for your body at Jesus' coming as Paul describes it in 1 Corinthians 15.

My body will become like Christ's glorified body. It will be whole, beautiful, glowing with the fullness of life. I will never experience trials or burdens in my body again. It will shine with the goodness of God's life.

Preparing the Body for Death and Resurrection: The Potter Molding the Clay

One way of understanding God as the great artist in creating human beings is to see Him as a great potter at the potter's wheel, molding His humans into vessels of stunning beauty and noble purpose.[13] Paul clearly conceives of God in this way in Romans 9: "You will say to me then, 'Why does He still find fault? For who can resist His will?' But who are you, O man, to answer back to God? Will what is molded say to its molder, 'Why have you made me like this?' Has the potter no right over the clay . . . ?" (vv. 19–21).

God's great pottery endeavor began in the Garden of Eden with His molding of a creature in His image and likeness. But human rebellion destructively marred the image. Still, God didn't relinquish His pottery work. Through Christ's death and resurrection, God has "turned death inside-out,"[14] and through the very thing that seeks to destroy the creature, God is at work, fashioning a new human being. As John Behr says:

Death will finally reveal in which direction my heart is oriented. However, until that point, it is still *I* who am doing this, dying to myself. When, on the other hand, *I* am finally returned to the dust, then *I* stop working. Then, and only then, do *I* finally experience my complete and utter frailty and weakness. Then, and only then, do *I* become clay (for *I* never was this), clay fashioned by the Hands of God into living flesh. And so, it is also only then that the God whose

---

13   This section is dependent upon the reflections of John Behr, *Becoming Human*.

14   Ibid., 46.

strength is made perfect in weakness can finally be the Creator: taking dust from the earth which I now am and mixing in His power, he now, finally, fashions a true, living human being—"the glory of God." When this happens, the act begun in Baptism is completed, and so, too, is the Eucharist.[15]

Our entire lives are the staging ground for God's great work in our own deaths: to become clay in the hands of our Creator and to be fashioned by Him after the image of the one true living human being: His Son, Jesus Christ. Death and resurrection are the great pottery wheel of God. Paul says this of the staging ground that is earthly life:

> But we have this treasure in jars of clay, to show that the surpassing power belongs to God and not to us. We are afflicted in every way, but not crushed; perplexed, but not driven to despair; persecuted, but not forsaken; struck down, but not destroyed; always carrying in the body the death of Jesus, so that the life of Jesus may also be manifested in our bodies. For we who live are always being given over to death for Jesus' sake, so that the life of Jesus also may be manifested in our mortal flesh. So death is at work in us, but life in you. (2 Corinthians 4:7–12)

Our death and resurrection is the opportunity for the Great Potter's final artistry.

QUESTIONS FOR DISCUSSION

How is it helpful for you to describe God as the great potter molding your body and life?

Our heavenly Father is in control and does everything through His Son. He is not finished with us yet. The pottery that is our bodies He will mold throughout this life, putting on the final glaze that is Jesus Christ at His coming. Nothing can separate us from His ongoing work at the potter's wheel. He will complete His artistic work: us!

How do you feel about becoming clay at your death for God to fashion into living flesh?

---

15   Ibid., 68–69.

Physical death is not something we embrace. But knowing that we are clay in God's hands through death can bring great comfort as we realize that our bodies and those of our faithful loved ones rest in the hands of our wise, loving, redeeming God. We can be confident in God's love and look forward with great excitement to the glorious way He will re-form our bodies into the beautiful living beings that He had intended at the beginning of creation.

Preparing for Death and Resurrection: Our Baptismal Body

If death and resurrection are the last act in the Trinity's great work of fashioning living human beings who are the corporate Body of Christ, then we are tasked in earthly life with preparing our bodies for death and resurrection. Both Baptism and the Lord's Supper serve as primary crucibles through which God molds and prepares us. In the waters we put on what might be called the baptismal body. The dying and rising of Baptism daily shapes this body until our final Baptism comes when our body is laid in its grave. Paul speaks of this baptismal body in Ephesians 4:20–24:

> But that is not the way you learned Christ!—assuming that you have heard about Him and were taught in Him, as the truth is in Jesus, to put off your old self, which belongs to your former manner of life and is corrupt through deceitful desires, and to be renewed in the spirit of your minds, and to put on the new self, created after the likeness of God in true righteousness and holiness.

So how have we learned Christ? How does Christ live out His life in and through us? As we put on the new self, Christ lives through us. Putting off our old self and putting on the new, shedding the skin of the sinner and donning the skin of the new person in Christ, is not just an act of the mind. It entails practicing disciplines that can help prepare the body for its final death and resurrection: fasting, abstinence, devotion, intense prayer, focused study of the Word, keeping vigil, austerity, and so forth. Through such disciplines we seek to destroy our misplaced hope in this body and this life, which is passing away, and focus our hope on the resurrected body and the life that is to come through the rule and reign of God. Luther described living in the baptismal body in the section on Baptism in the Small Catechism:

What does such baptizing with water signify? It indicates that the Old Adam in us should by daily contrition and repentance be drowned and die with all sins and evil desires, and that a new man should daily emerge and arise to live before God in righteousness and purity forever.[16]

As we live in our baptismal bodies, God is molding us for the final turn of the potter's wheel: our death and resurrection.

QUESTIONS FOR DISCUSSION

How do you shed your old skin and put on your new skin in Christ?
We shed the old skin through Baptism and in our return to Baptism through repentance, that is, turning from our old, self-centered manner of living to live in a new way—a new outlook, a new obedience worked in us by the Holy Spirit. We put on faith and the new obedience—the fruits of the Spirit that flow from faith. That is putting on a new skin in Christ.

Tell about a discipline that helps to prepare your body for its final death and resurrection, or identify one that you might like to adopt.
There are many ways to remind ourselves that our bodies live only in the hope of the resurrected life of Jesus. Fasting prepares us to long for the living food of the feast of God's new earth.

Abstaining from any of the pleasures of this earthly life prepares us for the divine pleasures we will find in the new heavens and the new earth.

Exercise prepares us to live within the limitations of our present earthly body—our strength, our lung capacity, our stamina and endurance—and points us toward the day when our bodies will be naturally exercised through our life in the new heaven and new earth.

These are only examples among many disciplines.

---

16   *Luther's Small Catechism with Explanation* (St. Louis: Concordia Publishing House, 2017), 24.

Preparing for Death and Resurrection:
Our Corporate, Eucharistic Body

God's task is not only to re-create individual living human beings, but also, in Christ, He is creating one complete and whole corporate body of human people, one great family of humans. This body takes its final shape in the eternal banquet feast of the Lamb in His kingdom. The preparation for participation in this great eucharistic (thanksgiving) body is the Church's weekly celebration of the Supper of the Lord, the Holy Eucharist.

The spiritual body that will rise on the final day will be nurtured eternally, not primarily by physical food, but by the Word of God. As Jesus said during His temptation in the wilderness, "It is written, 'Man shall not live by bread alone, but by every word that comes from the mouth of God'" (Matthew 4:4). The Lord's Supper gives us this living Word of God in bread and wine that sustains our bodies as they make the pilgrimage through physical death to resurrection in the rule and reign of God.

Participation in the Supper shapes our own bodies to live toward the hope of Christ's coming: "As often as you eat this bread and drink the cup, you proclaim the Lord's death until He comes" (1 Corinthians 11:26). This was the experience of the disciples on the road to Emmaus when they encountered the risen Christ. As Jesus celebrated the Lord's Supper with them, their eyes were opened and they recognized Him and saw themselves as included in His story and in His kingdom. Even though our bodies will die and lie in the ground, we treasure and nurture our bodies because of the glory that will be revealed in them as they participate in Jesus' story of resurrection to eternal life.

So, through Baptism and the Lord's Supper, we ready ourselves for the final act of the Great Potter, for each of us in our individual body and for all of us together as one resurrected Body of Christ.

QUESTIONS FOR DISCUSSION

Describe what Paul means in 1 Corinthians 11:26 in your own words.

Every time I eat this bread and drink this cup, the crucified and risen body and blood of the Lord, I confess that I have life only in God's name by His death, resurrection, ascension, and return to establish His kingdom. I confess that His reign through His death and resurrection is the only desired life and future for me and all who receive His body and blood. I confess that after my death in my flesh, I shall see God (Job 19:25–26) because I have received the body and blood of the One who has conquered death.

When you participate in the Lord's Supper, how does it help you to see the whole Body of Christ, one corporate body of persons, and to love all who are in that body?

As Paul says in 1 Corinthians 10:17, we all partake of the one bread and so are one body. We also participate in the one cup. Eating from the one bread and the one cup makes us one in the Christ whose bread and cup it is. Eating together that common bread and cup means that we all participate in the same Lord Jesus and through His body and blood are made one body in Him. We see it as we all share in the same consecrated loaf and blessed cup.

Conclusion

As Luther says in the explanation to the First Article of the Apostles' Creed in the Small Catechism, God has made you and all creatures and has given you your body and soul, eyes, ears, and all your members, your reason and all your senses, and still takes care of them.[17]

Your body, as part of the person God created, is His gift to you. God has given all of us the gift of our bodies, and we live together bodily in this world. God in Christ is restoring us, personally and corporately—restoring our bodies and our common bodily life, as Paul says: "There is one body and one Spirit—just as you were called to the one hope that belongs to your call—one Lord, one faith, one baptism, one God and Father of all, who is over all and through all and in all" (Ephesians 4:4–6).

On the Last Day the triune God will raise your body from the grave and you will enter bodily into the rule and reign of God in Christ Jesus, the incarnate, crucified, and resurrected one. The rest of your life is a staging ground to prepare you and your body for your death and your dying and for the new

---

17   *Luther's Small Catechism with Explanation*, 16.

bodily life that will be yours at Jesus' coming. "He who calls you is faithful; He will surely do it" (1 Thessalonians 5:24).

We Praise You, Jesus, at Your Birth

1. We praise You, Jesus at Your birth;
   Clothed in flesh You came to earth.
   The virgin bears a sinless boy
   And all the angels sing for joy.
   Alleluia!

2. Now in the manger we may see
   God's Son from eternity,
   The gift from God's eternal throne
   Here clothed in our poor flesh and bone.
   Alleluia!

3. The virgin Mary's lullaby
   Calms the infant Lord Most High.
   Upon her lap content is He
   Who keeps the earth and sky and sea.
   Alleluia!

4. The Light Eternal, breaking through,
   Made the world to gleam anew;
   His beams have pierced the core of night,
   He makes us children of the light.
   Alleluia!

5. The very Son of God sublime
   Entered into earthly time
   To lead us from this world of cares
   To heaven's courts as blessed heirs.
   Alleluia!

6. In poverty He came to earth
   Showering mercy by His birth;
   He makes us rich in heav'nly ways
   As we, like angels, sing His praise.
   Alleluia!

7. All this for us our God has done
   Granting love through His own Son.
   Therefore, all Christendom, rejoice
   And sing His praise with endless voice.
   Alleluia!

Text: German, ca. 1830, st. 1; Martin Luther, 1483–1546, sts. 2–7; tr. Gregory J. Wismar, b. 1946, sts. 1, 6; tr. F. Samuel Janzow, 1913–2001, sts. 2, 4, u. *Lutheran Service Book*, 2006, sts. 3, 5, 7. Sts. 1, 3, 5–7 © 2006 Concordia Publishing House; sts. 2, 4 © 1978 Concordia Publishing House.

CHAPTER 2

YOUR DEATH, YOUR DYING

Introduction

> [Jacob] commanded them [his sons] and said to them, "I
> am to be gathered to my people; bury me with my fathers in
> the cave that is in the field of Ephron the Hittite, . . . in the
> land of Canaan, which Abraham bought with the field from
> Ephron the Hittite to possess as a burying place. There they
> buried Abraham and Sarah his wife. There they buried Isaac
> and Rebekah his wife, and there I buried Leah." . . . When
> Jacob finished commanding his sons, he drew up his feet into
> the bed and breathed his last and was gathered to his people.
> (Genesis 49:29–31, 33)

What is it about death that scares us? What causes us to ignore it, for the
most part, until death stares us in the face? Our culture tells us death is just
part of life, or that it is natural, but that is not how the Bible speaks about
death.

Death was not part of God's creation. God was meticulous in His creating
act. He formed us from the dust of the earth to live, specifically, with Him.
Picture this for a moment: God the Creator of the universe gets down on His
hands and knees to form you. Then He breathes the breath of life into your
body to give you life. John Baillie says it best: "Thou, O Lord God . . . hast
breathed into me the breath of Thine own life."[18]

If this is not the beginning of a personal, intimate relationship, what is?
"Then the Lord God formed the man of dust from the ground and breathed
into his nostrils the breath of life, and the man became a living creature" (Genesis 2:7). Here are some of the most intimate words of Scripture. We were created to be in relationship with our Creator.

---

18   John Baillie, *A Diary of Private Prayer* (New York: Charles Scribner's Sons, 1949), 65.

But we all know what happened next. The man and woman decided that this amazing relationship with the Creator of the universe was not enough. They allowed Satan to convince them that their advancement was more important than any relationship with God, and they ate the fruit of the tree. Immediately, they knew everything had changed. And in their eating, they ripped their relationship with each other, the creation, and the Creator into a million pieces. The result of destroying this relationship was and is death!

So, death is not what God had planned for His creatures. It was never meant to be "a part of life." Death is our enemy. It's an enemy we hold at a distance and an enemy we would rather not deal with. Death is division, separation, and an unsure reality rolled into one.

I believe the reason death scares us is because we have no control over it. We can't stop it, we can't determine when it will happen[19] (or at least we shouldn't), and we certainly don't understand what happens when death occurs. Yet, on this earth, death happens every single day, every hour, and every second, and it will happen to every single one of us.

Most of us are curious about death, especially when someone dies, but it is not one of those day-to-day conversations we share with others. So, let's bring it to the table for discussion.

QUESTIONS FOR DISCUSSION

What is it about death that makes it hard to talk about?
Consider your own experiences with death—grandparents, parents, friends, even pets.

What is it that you fear about death?
Do you fear the unknown nature of death and what lies beyond that moment? Do you fear the helplessness of death? Is it the idea of a terminal illness with its pain or wasting away? Do you fear the loss of control?

How have you planned for your death?
Some prepare wills with directives for who will raise their children. Others have health-care directives. Some set up a trust or choose a cemetery.

---

19   There have been many times, and many more will come, when our culture has fought for and defended euthanasia, physician-assisted suicide, for our loved ones. You may have considered taking your own life. But our lives are a gift of the Creator. We don't get to decide when to die. These decisions not only negate Church practice, but also God's sovereign will. He created each of us and He loves us, and we should never determine our own death.

How does thinking about death affect the way you live your life?

Thinking about death reminds us not to take our day-to-day lives for granted—which we so easily do. It also makes us see life's true priorities—relationships with God, with our loved ones, family, and friends.

The Act of Dying

Have you ever been present in the days or hours before a loved one dies? Dying is a process, both medically and spiritually.[20] Of course, spiritual death seems less obvious, especially when a tragic death occurs, but even then, there is likely some sort of reflection that takes place. This "act" of dying becomes much more obvious when a terminally ill patient dies. Yet, this process is visible even in those with short-term illnesses and those who are aged.

As my mother lay dying, there were days that seemed as if she were frozen in time. She didn't get better, but she didn't worsen. I vividly remember my mother asking, "When will He come for me? Why must I wait so long?" Of course, I had no answer. I really knew nothing about the act of dying. My mother's act of dying, to the best of my recollection, lasted roughly two weeks. She took her last breath early in the morning on January 27, 2010.

My father has also died. His last breath was early morning on August 18, 1998. I was present when both my parents died, but they were very different experiences. My father didn't discuss death per se; it was happening, and that was it. His death was much more dignified—less personal and more matter-of-fact. He died the way he lived: a private man, but a man filled with a very deep faith. Don't misunderstand me; he loved us all dearly, but he was a German man raised with the understanding that the way you care for those you love is less about emotional connections and more through putting food on the table. I believe, and know for a fact, he was much different with my mother. He loved her with every fiber of his being. Of course he loved his children dearly, but his love for my mother was a much more visible love.

---

20   When we discuss spiritual death here, we mean the spiritual dimension of death, the moment our spirit, our soul, our being—whatever you want to name it—meets Christ. According to Jesus' word, only the Christian will experience this kind of spiritual death. A non-Christian will experience hell, which could be considered a spiritual death, but that will not be the language used here.

I had flown in from Phoenix to be with him. On my way to the hospital, I picked up his favorite meal: beef tenderloin wrapped in bacon. He loved this meal. He nibbled at it but really didn't eat much. That afternoon as he and I were alone in his hospital room, we talked briefly about a lot of things, including his dying. I shared with him how much I loved him and that I would miss him dearly. I left that afternoon knowing he was in the act of dying. On the day I was booked to return to Phoenix, we got the call from our mother that Dad had taken a turn for the worse. My brother-in-law and I got in the car and headed to the hospital. That final day as he lay dying, I remember his entire family being there in the hospital, but I don't remember him ever gathering us all together at one time. In some ways, his death reflected his life with small, personal, intimate relationships, but recalling he never really liked huge family gatherings. My father was a man of deep faith. He served God through loving and serving his family.

On the other hand, my mother's death was intimate, much more intimate. Her family was there most of the time, and throughout the days before she died, we came and went. One night, roughly forty-eight hours before she died, she asked that I invite everyone into the room.

At this point, she was receiving a morphine shot about every four hours, but for some reason this evening the nurse did not come, and my mother's pain seemed to have subsided. She was joyful, laughing, and talking up a storm. She talked about dating as a young girl, about her parents and brother, and about meeting my father.

For hours, it seemed, she was able to sit up, to talk and laugh. She answered questions from her children and grandchildren. It was an evening that we will never forget. It was as if for just that moment in time, she wasn't actually dying. There was laughter, joy, and an amazing peace throughout the room.

When she finally tired, everyone left the room except me, as it was my night to stay with her. I was honored that it was my turn to stay with her. We spoke briefly, and then I moved over to a couch to rest. Thinking back, I wish I had never moved that far away from her, as she was restless that night and woke often. Her pain level increased throughout the evening and a nurse came in and provided some relief.

Around 2 a.m., she woke me, asked for water, and told me she would love some chocolate ice cream. I laughed and, determined to find it, headed out.

Fifteen minutes later, she enjoyed a small dish of chocolate ice cream. I remember she didn't eat it all, but she truly enjoyed each bite. Early the next morning I sat on her bed and together we prayed Luther's Morning Prayer and the Lord's Prayer.

When the nurses changed shifts around 6 a.m., Mom was tired and in pain, and I knew the end was drawing near. The four-hour doses of morphine were not enough, and the nurse switched Mom to a constant morphine drip. With it she slowly drifted into what seemed like a drug-induced coma. That was it—no more smiles, no more conversation, no more laughter . . . just slow, steady breathing. I contacted my sisters and they returned to the hospital. We also contacted my brothers by phone and updated them on Mom's condition.

I still have a vivid image of my mother's final hours. An oxygen tube properly placed around both ears and attached through her nose gave a slowed but steady inhaling of oxygen. She was alive throughout the day, but soon after midnight, she took her final breath and was gone.

It was a quiet death, but it was certainly a process, one that is still alive in my mind. The process lasted for days. At times she was comforted and at other times frustrated—frustrated by the act of dying. She had days of lucidity and days of quiet intoxication. She was loved and she knew God loved her and that He would take her home. Some would say she died a beautiful death, but death is not beautiful in any way, because someone dies and those left behind are full of pain and sorrow.

If I was asked to use a single word to describe both of my parents' deaths, I would say they were peaceful. Both of them knew and were comforted by the fact that God was in control. As I think back, both of my parents gave all control over to God. Maybe that is why my memories of my father's death seem so private; he trusted and knew that his Creator was with him through it all.

Dying is a process. We experience it every single day. It may be slow and long or it may be quick and happen in an instant, but it will happen. All of us will experience the process of death unless Christ returns first.

QUESTIONS FOR DISCUSSION

If you've experienced the dying process with someone, what you do remember? Is there anything you would like to share?

If you've been present during someone's death, what part of the dying process was peaceful? What parts were hard?

If you could have done something differently, what might it have been?

Opening Discussion about Death

How do we begin to talk about death? How do we conform our lives now so that we will be ready to give all control over to God when we personally encounter death? Let's start where Scripture starts, with God's solemn warning to the first humans in the Garden of Eden: "But of the tree of the knowledge of good and evil you shall not eat, for in the day that you eat of it you shall surely die" (Genesis 2:17).

Then Satan comes with his manipulating words: "You will not surely die" (Genesis 3:4). The master of lies plays his trump card and humanity falls for it. We eat and we die. It's at this point in Scripture when the death of all God's human creatures begins to be recorded: "Adam lived . . . 930 years, and he died" (Genesis 5:5); "all the days of Seth were 912 years, and he died" (v. 8); "all the days of Enosh were 905 years, and he died" (v. 11). On and on throughout the Bible, God's children live and they die.

That refrain goes unbroken until the seventh generation and a man named Enoch. "All the days of Enoch were 365 years. Enoch walked with God, and he was not, for God took him" (Genesis 5:23–24). Where did God take Enoch? He took him to Himself. God reached down and snatched a man from the jaws of death. God spared Enoch from death to give us the first glimpse of what lies beyond death for a child of God—ongoing life with God after our earthly life is over.

But aside from that glimmer of hope, the Bible does not tell us much about death. It does tell us that we will certainly die and that the Lord Himself has total control over both our life and death: "The Spirit of God has made me, and the breath of the Almighty gives me life" (Job 33:4). "When You hide Your face, they [God's creatures] are dismayed; when You take away their breath, they die and return to their dust" (Psalm 104:29). Isaac told his son Esau, "Behold, I am old; I do not know the day of my death" (Genesis 27:2).

God, our Creator, is in control of our life and our death. But God has given us hope in the face of death. In life, in this time and place, we are reunited with the Creator through the life and death of His Son, Jesus Christ. Because of that union we will also be united with Him in our death. "For the wages of sin is death, but the free gift of God is eternal life in Christ Jesus our Lord" (Romans 6:23).

Let's begin the discussion about death with the realization that death will take place. It will happen. It cannot be avoided. But we, God's children, live with the hope of eternal life promised by Christ, and if our discussion is centered on this reality, then death becomes less fearful and the topic opens for discussion.

Now, this is not to ignore the fact that death is painful, extremely painful. It tears at the core of our being. It confuses, disorients, and breaks the hearts of those left behind. In fact, it is one of the most painful realities of life. We will deal with this personal reality at greater length in chapter 3. But for now, let's just open up a discussion about death.

QUESTIONS FOR DISCUSSION

Have you thought about your own death?

Different life events can lead us to contemplate our own death—the death of loved ones, a close brush on the highway, serious surgery, awaiting the results of hospital tests.

If yes, what do you think about? If no, why not?

Do you find death comforting, disturbing, or something else?

Understanding Death: Medically

"Acknowledging the dead would mean accepting one's own mortality."[21]

How might we come to understand death and deal with dying when Scripture provides little to guide us? It may become easier to understand if we start by medically defining death. By doing this we will understand that death is a process, not something instantaneous.

---

21   Kenneth V. Iserson, *Death to Dust: What Happens to Dead Bodies?* (Tucson, AZ: Galen Press, Ltd., 1994), 3.

Even after the breath of life has gone and the heart has stopped beating, the body still goes through the process of dying. For up to three hours after death, a person's pupils still respond to certain stimuli. For up to twenty-four hours, the skin can still be a viable graft for donation, and for up to forty-eight hours, a person's bones can still be a viable graft for donation.[22] Science helps us understand how death can also become a gift of life.[23]

Medically speaking, when does a person die? For years, a person was declared dead when the heart stopped beating, but that changed when science discovered cardiopulmonary resuscitation (CPR) as a way to restart the heart. Surgeons have even discovered ways to intentionally stop and restart the heart in order to repair it or remove and replace it. So we can no longer consider the stopping of the heart to be an accurate determiner of death.

For thousands of years, including today, people have feared being declared dead when they really weren't. How did the culture and the medical field deal with this? Here is a brief historical overview. Ancient Greeks and Romans waited for a body to decay for three or five days before committing it to burial or cremation. The Romans went so far as cutting off a finger to see if it bled before consigning a body to the funeral pyre. Celts watched over their dead at home for a period of time, checking regularly to see if life might return. Jews, in a similar way, watched over their dead by placing them in unsealed sepulchers for up to three days. During these days, relatives were given the responsibility of daily visiting the tomb to keep watch but also in the hope that life and breath might return to their loved one.

In Shakespeare's *Henry IV*, he recorded two ancient methods for detecting death: the use of a feather and the use of a mirror. A feather was placed below the nose to detect any movement of air from exhaling or inhaling. In a similar fashion, a mirror was used to detect a mist or "stain" of breath. For hundreds of years, especially beginning around the fourteenth century, there were stories of people leaving notes with specific instructions to follow before declaring them dead.

In the United States there were old wives' tales about declaring someone

---

22   Penny Colman, *Corpses, Coffins, and Crypts: A History of Burial* (New York: Henry Holt and Company, 1997).

23   To find out more about organ donation, consider this website: https://organdonor.gov/about/what.html. If you want to understand more about whole body donation, a helpful website is http://www.sciencecare.com/.

dead. In the early nineteenth century, a doctor by the name of Jost won first prize at the Académie de France for inventing clawed forceps used to pinch a corpse's nipple. Even today, across all cultures, new ways of declaring death continue. One would think the introduction of arterial embalming between 1880 and 1890 would have eliminated all fears of being buried alive. If you weren't dead *before* the embalming process, you certainly were *after*, because embalming a body requires that all the blood be drained and replaced by injections of a lethal chemical.[24]

Because of medical advances enjoyed today, a different kind of problem has arisen. Respirators and other machines can keep the heart and circulation and almost every other organ of the human body properly functioning after the brain has died. The medical field has used the term *brain-dead* to describe "the inability of the whole organism, the person, to continue to function and independently regulate itself."[25] But when a person is pronounced brain dead and put on an artificial ventilator (sometimes called a respirator), it eliminates the traditional signs of death—the heartbeat ceasing and the person no longer breathing. This makes it much more difficult to pronounce someone dead.

Thinking of death from this perspective causes the medical field—and the Church, for that matter—to ask the question, What is the relationship between the human being and the body itself? This question has occupied the minds of philosophers, physicians, and the religious community throughout the ages. Two contradictory answers usually surface. The first is that of the "corporealists," those who view the human as nothing more than the body and the brain. In contrast, "dualists" view the body as purely incidental to pure reason and will.[26] We will tackle this question in greater depth from a religious perspective later in the chapter.

Defining death by brain function criteria means that the body is physiologically decapitated.27 Other parts of the body may continue to work—blood is circulating, the heart is pumping—but all brain activity has ceased and the person is irreversibly dead. Even this definition can be a bit ambiguous be-

---

24   Iserson, *Death to Dust*, 24–36.

25   Ibid., 14.

26   Ibid., 14–15.

27   Ibid., 15.

cause it refers to three distinct types of brain malfunction. In his book *Death to Dust: What Happens to Dead Bodies?*, Kenneth Iserson, MD, describes these types:

> (1) death by *whole brain criteria*, in which the entire brain and the brainstem have ceased functioning; (2) *cerebral death*, in which most sections of the brain have ceased functioning, but the lowest centers in the cerebellum (back of brain and brainstem) still function; and (3) *neocortical death*, in which there is a lack of function in the "thinking" part of the brain. Neocortical death is not recognized in the United States, Britain, Canada and most other countries that recognize death by brain criteria.[28]

Most countries, including the United States, accept "death by whole brain criteria" as the most accepted and only legal definition. It's described as complete loss of function in both the upper brain and the brain stem. Physicians describe the upper brain (the neocortex) as that which perceives pain and pleasure, holds one's thoughts, and controls one's actions; in medical terms, "it is the person." The brain stem, which is found at the base of the brain, controls all basic biological function. The brain stem must function for the upper brain to properly function. The brain stem controls breathing, blood pressure, and wakefulness. Everything passes through the brain stem. It is the pathway for movement of the entire body. "Once the brainstem is inoperative, the whole brain is dead."[29]

As Iserson's definition shows, the medical field attempts to establish irreversible loss of brain stem function. This is based on purely clinical grounds. The steps are as follows: "(1) determine the cause of a coma; (2) decide that irremediable structural brain damage has occurred; (3) eliminate reversible cause of coma such as extremely low body temperature, drug intoxication, or a severe chemical imbalance; and (4) demonstrate that all brain stem reflexes, including breathing, are absent."[30]

Although it is interesting to understand death medically, it brings no

---

28   Ibid.

29   Ibid., 16.

30   Ibid.

comfort. Death is something distant and sterile; it neither needs nor cares about the importance the Christian places on the body, the total being. Death as defined by the medical profession ends right there; there is little left to do but remove the body. But for the Christian, there is more to the story.

QUESTIONS FOR DISCUSSION

What did you learn from understanding death medically?

Many don't realize how complex and difficult it can be to determine actual medical death. You might begin the conversation by discussing what surprised you about medical death.

How did it make you feel to read about death from this perspective?

Medically declaring someone brain-dead can seem cold and callous. How might this contradict a Christian perspective?

From a Christian perspective, the body in its totality belongs to God. This is not how the medical profession views the body. Sometimes medicine acts as if all thoughts, memories, and perceptions take place in the brain, and thus when the brain is dead, these thoughts, memories, and perceptions cease to exist. But a Christian perspective puts thoughts, memories, and perceptions in the soul, which lives on after the body dies. That does not mean we will be concerned about loved ones we leave behind on earth. God will "wipe away every tear from [our] eyes" (Revelation 7:17), and we will enjoy perfect peace and joy in the presence of the Savior.

Does understanding death from a medical perspective make death feel more distant, or does it make it more understandable?

Understanding Death: A Christian Perspective

To begin the Christian discussion of death, let's return to the question asked earlier: What is the relationship between the human being and the body itself? This will be the template for reflecting on death. Why is this an important question, and why has this question occupied the minds of theologians, philosophers, and physicians alike for thousands of years?

From a Christian perspective, and as we have seen from the first chapter, the Church acknowledges and recognizes the importance of the body but also that we are much more than just physical bodies. We are creaturely embodied beings. In theological terms, we must ask the question, What does it mean to be a living human being or a human creature?

First and foremost, it begs us to recognize that we are created, not by our own power, but by the power or hand of the Creator. This act of creation brings us into a relationship with the Creator. Let's return to Genesis: "Then the Lord God formed man of dust from the ground, and breathed into his nostrils the breath of life; and man became a living being." So man, the human creature, the living being, is but dust and breath. Or as Chuck Arand[31] has coined, "I am a breath-enlivened body."[32]

Sometimes from a worldly perspective, even a medical perspective, we hear that our bodies are unimportant, that they are but shells, but that is not how the Bible speaks. We are living human beings, created to be in relationship—with each other, with God, and with His creation. Thomas Long in *Accompany Them with Singing: The Christian Funeral* says:

> Christians, to sum it up, do not believe that human beings are *only* bodies, nor do they believe that they are souls who, for the time being, *have* bodies; Christians affirm, rather, that human beings are *embodied.* What others call "the soul" and "the body," Christians call the "breath of God" and dust; and when it comes to living human beings, they form an inseparable unity.[33]

We are not just a body, nor are we a soul living in a body; we are creatures created by God. Our lives are a gift from God. But "take away the breath of God, and there is no immortal soul left over to make a break for it to freedom; there is just dust."[34] "In the sweat of your face you shall eat bread, till you return to

---

31 Dr. Charles Arand has been on the faculty of Concordia Seminary, St. Louis, since 1989. He is an esteemed professor of Systematic Theology. In addition, he is the dean of Theological Research and Publication and director of the Center for the Care of Creation. His area of expertise includes the Lutheran Confessions and the theology of creation.

32 Chuck Arand, "I Am God's Creature! Luther's Confession of the First Article of the Creed" (unpublished article), 9.

33 Thomas G. Long, *Accompany Them with Singing: The Christian Funeral* (Louisville, KY: Westminster John Knox, 2009), 24.

34 Ibid., 24.

the ground, for out of it you were taken; you are dust, and to dust you shall return" (Genesis 3:19).

Scripture speaks of man in a myriad of ways. Isaiah 10:18 and Matthew 10:28 speak of the human consisting of body and soul. In 1 Corinthians 5:5, Paul speaks of man being flesh and spirit; Romans 7:25 speaks of mind and flesh. It can also be referred to as consisting of spirit, soul, and body, as in 1 Thessalonians 5:23. But that is not all. Other passages, such as Genesis 2:7, speak of man as a unitary being. Since all of these are scriptural, all need to be affirmed and defended.[35]

This begs the question, What makes the human creature unique? What sets him or her apart from the beasts of the field and the birds of the air? Again, let's look back at Genesis and see what the difference is between the creation of man and the rest of creation. On the fifth day, God brought forth "swarms of living creatures" in the waters and across the firmament of heaven (Genesis 1:20). On the sixth day, from the earth, He directed the earth to "bring forth living creatures according to their kinds—livestock and creeping things and beasts of the earth" (v. 24). Then, in verse 30, God showed us that He has given the breath of life to every created being. In this, all God's created animal kingdom has the breath of life, just like the human creature.

But in verse 26, we see a few things that make the human creature different from the animals. Here God says, "Let Us make man in Our image, after Our likeness. And let them have dominion over the fish of the sea and over the birds of the heavens and over the livestock and over all the earth and over every creeping thing that creeps on the earth." Genesis 2:19 confirms this fact: "Now out of the ground the LORD God had formed every beast of the field and every bird of the heavens and brought them to the man to see what he would call them."

Both human creatures and animal creatures are formed of the dust of the earth, but there is an intimacy in the creation of man in Genesis 1:26 and 2:7: "Let us make man in Our image, after Our likeness. And let them have dominion over the fish of the sea and over the birds of the heavens and over the livestock and over the all the earth and over every creeping thing that creeps

---

35   Report of the Commission on Theology and Church Relations (CTCR), *A Statement on Death, Resurrection, and Immortality* (The Lutheran Church—Missouri Synod, 1969).

on the earth. . . . Then the LORD God formed the man of dust from the ground and breathed into his nostrils the breath of life, and the man became a living creature." So, the creation of man differs from the creation of the rest of God's created beings in three unique and special ways:

1. Man was created in the image and after the likeness of God.

2. Man was given dominion over the created animals.

3. God breathed into the nostrils of man the breath of life. This is another unique characteristic that needs to be dealt with in much greater detail.

There can be no denying that there is something unique, something different, about man's relationship to God. Might there then be something different, something unique, in our dying? Here is normally where the topic of the image of God and the soul arises.

QUESTIONS FOR DISCUSSION

In your own words, describe the soul.

Luther describes the soul as "my reason and all my senses." Many others would describe it as our mind and spirit, or our breath that gives life to our body.

Do you believe the human being has a soul?

Do you believe having a soul is what sets humans apart from the animals?

Many people believe this. (Check the text of Genesis.) This works if the breath of life is how the humans received their soul.

What do you think happens to the soul when someone dies?

Is the soul connected with the image or the likeness of God?

The Soul

When it comes to discussing the soul, at least for the Christian, death becomes a much more intimate and personal topic. Yet, the Christian tradition has long defined this topic from a philosophical understanding. For thousands of years, when the Church spoke about the soul, it described it as something unique, something sacred, or something spiritual that only the human creature possesses. It has been described as immortal while the body itself is mortal. It has been described as incorruptible while the body is corruptible. You may have even heard that the physical body seeks the pleasures of the flesh while the soul seeks those things that are spiritual or of higher value to God. But that is not how the Bible speaks of the soul. So, what is the soul? Where does it come from? Can it be explained?

Let's begin this discussion by first understanding that much of our Christian traditional thought in regard to understanding body and soul has been influenced by philosophy. This is not a bad thing, but it must be recognized and acknowledged. Here is a short but vital historical perspective of philosophical influence on the Early Christian Church.

Soon after the destruction of the temple around AD 70 and the disruption of Judean autonomy between 132 and 135, the Christian movement, having some organized momentum, began to find its identity in the midst of heavy-handed Roman law. It was at about this time that the lines between orthodoxy and heterodoxy began to be drawn. The greatest distinction was between the Christian community and philosophy.

Philosophy departed sharply from many central truths of the Christian Church, and yet had a great influence on it, with one of its central questions focused on the nature of the body and soul. Philosophy taught ideas like, the body is evil material matter and it holds captive—or better yet, imprisons—the soul of each individual. Thus, each individual's goal was to save the soul from this imprisonment and release it from the evil material matter of the body. Or that each human being is composed essentially of a nonmaterial and immortal soul, which is temporarily housed in a disposable and usually loathsome body. Philosophy so penetrated the Church that at one point the body was viewed as profane while the soul was seen as divine. Many of these thoughts still exist and can be heard among Christians today.

But as we discussed in chapter 1, the Bible states that God honors the body He created and will raise and glorify that body on the Last Day, just as Christ's body was raised. For this reason, the Church also ought to honor and love the body.

So let's back up a bit and recognize that, first and foremost, we are creatures created by God, and second, we are mortal beings. We are not immortal; only

God is. We will live forever because of God, not because of some innate power in our soul.

Christians also reject the reductionist view that teaches that human beings are *just* bodies. This includes the idea that God created a human being (a mere body), then snatched some immortal soul out of the air and shoved it into that body. No, God tenderly and lovingly created the whole human being. From the dust of the earth God formed the human body and then breathed into it the breath of life. Only then did it become a living being. That is the biblical account.

To sum it all up, Christians do not believe they are *only* bodies, nor that they are only souls that *have* bodies for now. Rather, we confirm that we are embodied beings, either understood as body and soul or as the "breath of life" and dust. This embodied being is the creature God created

When Paul speaks to the Christians about putting on immortality (1 Corinthians 15:53), he is not speaking in a platonic way or about putting off the body to let the immortal soul soar free; he is preaching about the resurrection of the body, which returns us to the unique relational bond God has with His people. Nothing, including death, will separate us from God. "The trumpet will sound, and the dead will be raised imperishable" (v. 52). This highlights and should excite the Christian's understanding, because embodied mortals are being given new life in their glorified bodies and eternal life in the new creation by the grace and mercy of God.

So what language or what word shall we use to describe the soul? For thousands of years, people have used poetry, art, hymns, and the like to try and put language to work understanding the soul. In the well-known hymn "How Great Thou Art" (*LSB* 801), which Carl Boberg wrote as a poem in 1885, the refrain causes one to exude joy and gratefulness to God through the expression "then sings my soul."

Or take the hymn "When Peace, like a River" (*LSB* 763). The author, Horatio G. Spafford, following the Chicago fire in 1871 and the death of his only son at age 4, decided to move his wife and daughters to Europe. When he was detained in New York for business, he sent his wife and their four daughters on ahead. On November 22, 1873, during the small hours of the morning, the ship collided with a shipping vessel, and within two hours the ship had vanished along with Horatio's four daughters. His wife was found nearly unconscious, one of forty-seven survivors. Horatio immediately booked passage to meet his wife. As he passed over the possible wreckage site, he said to himself, "It is well; the will of God be done." From there the hymn with its peaceful refrain "It is well with my soul" evolved into what we sing today.[36] Here we hear the pains of sorrow, yet an amazing trust in God.

Both hymns use the language of the soul to praise God in joy and in sadness. But the soul is not an isolated disembodied being in either example; it is the entire embodied human being engaged.

Here are a couple of ways we might begin to talk about the soul. There can be no doubt that God has given us, His creatures, a soul. Jesus Himself says, "And do not fear those who kill the body but cannot kill the soul; rather fear Him who can destroy both soul and body in hell" (Matthew 10:28). We, God's human creatures, possess a soul. It is a gift given by God.

The human creature is bound by space and time, but God is not. So our understanding and the language we use to define or explain the soul offers but a glimpse of its deeper reality. When we dig into discussions of things unknown or of which we are given little knowledge, even biblically, we must acknowledge that what we may know is nowhere near God's reality or understanding: "For My thoughts are not your thoughts, neither are your ways My ways, declares the LORD" (Isaiah 55:8). But if we try to understand the soul through our knowledge of Christ, His life, death, and resurrection, we are at least grounded in a solid foundation.

I suggest we also consider viewing the soul from two different realities or perspectives: one from above, God's perspective devoid of time and space; and another from below, man's perspective, which is trapped in time and space. If we come to understand these two realities even a bit, we might have a chance to explain or at least understand more about the soul.

We previously discussed physical or bodily death from a medical perspective, but let's make sure we are clear from a Christian perspective. When we take our last breath, we die. Our physical body has exhausted all it has and we are dead. We can learn something about the death of our physical body by seeing how Christ breathed His last and died.

Texts from all four Gospels state this fact: "And Jesus cried out again with

---

36   Robert J. Morgan, *Then Sings My Soul* (Nashville: Thomas Nelson, 2003).

a loud voice and yielded up His spirit" (Matthew 27:50). "Jesus uttered a loud cry and breathed His last" (Mark 15:37). "Then Jesus, crying out with a loud voice, said, 'Father, into Your hands I commit My spirit!' And having said this He breathed His last" (Luke 23:46). "When Jesus had received the sour wine, He said, 'It is finished,' and He bowed His head and gave up His spirit" (John 19:30). The living, breathing Jesus has died. In each case, Jesus breathes His last and dies—and in Luke, He not only breathes His last, but He also commits His spirit to the Father. What might Luke be thinking?

From these texts, I think that in most cases, the words *breath* and *spirit* are used to describe the same act: death. When Jesus gives up His breath, or spirit, He dies. Jesus has died a physical death; His whole body has died. When we die we are no longer trapped in this time and space, and yet in that same moment of time, the Christian is totally and fully alive in Christ. "Truly, I say to you, today you will be with Me in paradise" (Luke 23:43). Something special, something unique, has transpired. We who are but breath-enlivened beings live on in Christ.

This life in Christ began the day we were baptized. Christ's death brought all creation and all mankind back into relationship with God. His death mended and restored the broken relationships of the past. So although we are dead, we are alive.

The Orthodox Church has also dealt with the body-soul dichotomy in a way that might provide some clarity. This dichotomy is understood in a unique and different way from what we normally hear. "Even in death the bodies of the saints reveal that, though still present in this world whilst awaiting the resurrection, they belong to the kingdom."[37] Jean-Claude Larchet points out that when a loved one dies, the body and soul are still united. "Spiritual life, which enables Christians to receive grace in the whole being (soul and body), has numerous positive effects on both. The body shares directly in the ordering, the unification, and the pacification that is established in the soul."[38]

Here the body and soul are uniquely and intricately bound together, and this remains even after death. In death, "the body is united to the soul in a different way, whilst remaining an integral part of the person."[39] Although

---

37   Larchet, *Theology of the Body,* 89.

38   Ibid., 87.

39   Ibid., 89.

Larchet is discussing the identity of saints, he is clear in his understanding of the connection of body and soul. "Here is further testimony to the fact that the body belongs to a person as one of the essential constituents of his or her being, that it exists in close union with the soul, that it fully participates in the spiritual life, and that it, too, is to be saved and deified."[40] Larchet uses "deified" not to say that man becomes God, but to confirm that the body is good and valued, the whole being.

We have grappled with how the body and soul can be understood throughout the Church, but what does the culture have to say about it? Is it important to even engage with the culture's understanding? I think that answer needs to be yes. Why? Because each of us lives in the culture, and because we live in the midst of the culture, we are daily affected—or at least influenced—by what the culture says and does. While we as Christians do our best not to listen to the culture, it does influence our thinking in more ways than we would like to acknowledge. It is best if we can make that acknowledgment and then sort through how it may or may not influence our thinking.

The Culture's Understanding of the Soul

Many in today's culture find Oprah Winfrey to be a guide of sorts to a wide array of topics. At one time she set out to ask a vast audience of people to explain or define the soul. Here are the answers she received:

- The soul is that which existed before you were born and will continue after you die.
- It is the "fingerprint" of God, which becomes the physical body.
- It is the core of one's being; it does not exist in space and time.
- It is the spirit, the connection one has to God; it is where the Holy Spirit resides.
- It's the spiritual essence of who we are.
- It is that which provides purpose for one's life.
- It is a part of us that never dies.
- It is who we are, our innermost being.

---

40   Ibid., 90.

- It is the consciousness of who you are beyond form.
- It is the indwelling consciousness that watches over the mind, our body, and our world.
- It's the center of one's being, the part of us that never changes.
- It has no form and exists everywhere.
- It is the truth of who we are, our life and our love.
- It is the divine part of our being.
- It is the part of us that is one with God.
- It is the immortal, eternal part of who we are as people; it will never die.
- It belongs to God.
- It is the lure of our becoming.[41]

As you can see, no two people describe the soul in the same way, but it is clear that most people believe it is that which is immortal and immaterial, and that the soul is distinct from the body.

But how do the Scriptures talk about the soul? How do the Lutheran Confessions speak of the soul? How did Luther discuss the soul? And what is the relationship that exists between death and the soul itself? These are the questions that come to mind when we ponder the relationship between the death of the body and its whole relationship to the human being.

Challenging Texts on the Soul

It can be said that however the soul exists, and in whatever form it resides, it is solely and purely a gift of the Creator Himself. In the context of death, biblical texts—in this case, from the Old Testament—discuss the soul in a couple of ways. First, the Old Testament frequently translates *nephesh*, "soul," as a synonym for "the total being." Second, the soul is that which is in relationship with or belongs to God. Let's take some time to grapple and wrestle with how both the Old and New Testament texts deal with the idea of the spirit.

Let's begin in Genesis 35:18, where Jacob's wife Rachel has suffered hard labor with the birth of her second son. After Rachel gave birth to Benjamin,

---

41   "What Is the Soul? Eckhart Tolle, Wayne Dyer and Others Define It," December 25, 2012, video, http://www.huffingtonpost.com/2012/12/25/what-is-the-soul-eckhart-tolle-wayne-dyer_n_2333335.html.

the text says, "As her soul [*nephesh* in Hebrew] was departing (for she died), she called his name Ben-oni; but his father called him Benjamin."[42] What might the text be pointing out here?

Recall from above that the Hebrew word *nephesh* is frequently translated as a synonym for "the total being." The word for "departing" mainly means to begin a journey. So in this case, does Genesis 35:18 refer to Rachel's spirit leaving her body or to Rachel as a total person leaving this life? The text is not clear. It could refer to Rachel departing this life, departing from Jacob, maybe departing to be with Christ. *Nephesh* can also be translated as "breath" or "spirit." But the same text is translated this way in the Jerusalem Bible: "At the moment when she breathed her last, for she was dying, she named him Ben-oni."

Other texts, such as the Psalms, provide us with an image of the soul returning to God. "Behold, the eye of the LORD is on those who fear Him, on those who hope in His steadfast love, that He may deliver their soul from death" (Psalm 33:18–19). Here the soul is being delivered, handed over, to the proper recipient. Could the text be highlighting a return to the Creator? Psalm 49:15 talks in a similar way: "But God will ransom my soul from the power of Sheol, for He will receive me." God receives the soul back to Himself, which in this psalm is "me." God receives me. Could my soul be the "me" God created? It has been translated as "my life."

Many other psalms focus on the deliverance of the soul, a returning and rescuing. "For You have delivered my soul from death, yes, my feet from falling, that I may walk before God in the light of life" (Psalm 56:13). "For You have delivered my soul from death, my eyes from tears, my feet from stumbling" (116:8).

In Isaiah, there is a calling or a returning of the creature to the Creator in order that the creature might live even though he or she has died. "Incline your ear, and come to Me; hear, that your soul may live; and I will make with you an everlasting covenant, My steadfast, sure love for David" (Isaiah 55:3). Here it seems clear that, somehow, we will live even when we have died.

Although none of these texts tells or explains to us what the soul exactly is, they all, in one way or another, relate the soul within the context of dying.

---

42   "In the Old Testament the soul is not conceived of as a separate entity from the body, with an existence of its own (as in Greek thought) but rather as the life, which here is slipping away." Derek Kidner, *Genesis: An Introduction and Commentary* (Downers Grove, IL: InterVarsity, 1967), 176.

Although the Old Testament does not give explicit witness to existence after death, it certainly does not deny it. Hosea provides a template for corporate preservation of all God's people. Hosea 6:2–3 states, "After two days He will revive us; on the third day He will raise us up, that we may live before Him." In a similar context, Hosea 13:14 promises, "I shall ransom them from the power of Sheol; I shall redeem them from Death." All of these texts point to redemption for the dead and the power of God's resurrection promise.

Let's take a look at Ecclesiastes, which has some interesting things to say about death. While some translations of Ecclesiastes 3, including the ESV, title the section "A Time for Everything," other translations, including the Jerusalem Bible, title it "Death."

Most of us have read or at least heard the opening verses of Ecclesiastes 3, which discuss that there is a time for everything. But let's move past this section and take a look at the beginning of the author's discussion about man and beast and even the death of each:

> The fate of man and beast is identical; one dies, the other too, and both have the selfsame breath; man has no advantage over the beast, for all is vanity. Both go to the same place; both originate from the dust and to the dust both return. Who knows if the spirit of man mounts upwards or if the spirit of the beast goes down to the earth? (Ecclesiastes 3:19–21, Jerusalem Bible)

We can't be sure exactly what the answer to that question is, but it certainly provides us with a text to grapple with. Another verse in Ecclesiastes to consider is 12:7 (again, from the Jerusalem Bible): "Before the dust returns to the earth as it once came from it, and the breath to God who gave it." The Jerusalem Bible footnote here is very intriguing: "The earthly part of man returns to earth. But since nothing on this earth can satisfy him, not all of him originates from earth, and that which is of God, returns to God." I think this becomes very helpful as we discuss that part of man that is not earthly. This connects us back to Genesis and the creation of man and woman when God breathes into man the breath of life.

In the New Testament, we have some similar renderings of the text. In Matthew 10:28, Jesus talks about a body and a soul: "And do not fear those who kill the body but cannot kill the soul. Rather fear Him who can destroy both soul and body in hell." In James 5:20, we read: "Let him know that whoever brings back a sinner from his wandering will save his soul from death." Consider also 1 Peter 2:11: "Beloved, I urge you as sojourners and exiles to abstain from the passions of the flesh, which wage war against your soul." Here the focus seems to be on discerning the dangers of focusing one's life solely on the fleshly or earthly things, and instead inclining one's thoughts to the heavenly things of God, but this is not speaking of the body and soul as two unique and different entities.

The text shows that Christ, the one who was bodily raised from the dead so that we might live, calls us back to Himself in a way similar to the manner in which Jacob was called into a relationship with God. Romans 8 explains it this way: "For those who live according to the flesh set their minds on the things of the flesh, but those who live according to the Spirit set their minds on the things of the Spirit. For to set the mind on the flesh is death, but to set the mind on the Spirit is life and peace" (vv. 5–6).

In 2 Corinthians 5, Paul discusses with the Corinthians the hope we have in Christ and the promise of our resurrected body, our body made new in Christ. Some have read this text as Paul wanting to be away from his physical body, which makes sense when we recall that for most of his time as a Christian, he had been persecuted. But as he states in 2 Corinthians 4:18, Paul focuses not on his afflictions but instead on God's promise and the hope he has in the resurrection of Christ.

Here we can also make direct connections to Romans 8:23: "And not only the creation, but we ourselves, who have the firstfruits of the Spirit, groan inwardly as we wait eagerly for adoption as sons, the redemption of our bodies." We also consider 1 Corinthians 15:53–54: "For this perishable body must put on the imperishable, and this mortal body must put on immortality. When the perishable puts on the imperishable, and the mortal puts on immortality, then shall come to pass the saying that is written: 'Death is swallowed up in victory.'"

Biblical texts talk often about a soul, but nowhere is it clearly defined. Maybe it is the image or likeness of God, or maybe it is something indescribable by humans; but it is clear that God created His creatures from the dust of the ground and the breath of life and that those who believe in Him shall never die. "From now on, therefore, we regard no one according to the flesh. Even though we once regarded Christ according to the flesh, we regard Him thus no longer. Therefore, if anyone is in Christ, he is a new creation. The old has passed away; behold the new has come" (2 Corinthians 5:16–17).

Martin Luther, in his explanation of the First Article of the Apostles' Creed, states, "[God] has given *me* my body and soul" (emphasis added).[43] The "me" is my body and soul, not two parts, but together in unity; they are the "me" God created. As Luther notes, he does not "love the head and hate the foot, nor favor the soul and hate the body."[44] We are created living beings. Luther then describes my body as "my eyes, ears, and all my members" and the soul as "my reason and all my senses." Here we might conclude that the body is my outside component or activity,[45] that which interacts with God's creation; and the soul is my inside component or activity, which perceives or understands the world.

This is very similar to the way in which the Athanasian Creed speaks of Christ as "a perfect human being composed of a rational soul and human flesh." This is the *me* God created. And if it is the *me* God created, then God rescues and delivers me in bodily form. God has created me in His image and likeness. When Christ rescued me, He rescued all of me, body and soul in totality. Nothing is left behind, nothing is separated.

In considering the soul, we can also lean upon Francis Pieper,[46] who says:

> These texts [Acts 7:59; Luke 23:44, 46] surely make it evident that the departed souls of the believers are in a state of blessed enjoyment of God, even though we know nothing further as to the manner of their blessed communion with God. Deductions from the nature of the soul, e.g., that it cannot be inactive, are uncertain and therefore not to be urged in theology.[47]

---

43   *Luther's Small Catechism with Explanation*, 16.

44   LW 32:228.

45   Arand, 10.

46   Francis Pieper was the fourth president of The Lutheran Church—Missouri Synod. Born in Germany in June 1852, he immigrated to the United States in 1870 and five years later graduated from Concordia Seminary in St. Louis. He served as a pastor in Wisconsin until 1878, when he was called as a professor at Concordia Seminary, St. Louis. In 1887 he became seminary president and served until being called as the synod's president in 1899, where he served until 1911. Pieper is the author of *Christliche Dogmatik*, which he wrote during 1917–24 and which was later translated into English as *Christian Dogmatics*. It is a three-volume set still used at both seminaries.

47   Francis Pieper, *Christian Doctrine*, vol. 3 (St. Louis: Concordia, 1953), 512.

The soul may not be something that we see, but we live in the belief that Christ's death and resurrection promises us eternal life and that although we have died, we live.

A Christian's death reveals two stark and valid realities. First, it is abundantly clear that our loved one has died. Breath and life no longer reside in that Christian brother or sister. Death, our enemy, has claimed yet another life. But Christ changes this reality for the Christian. Easter changes this reality. Christ "unmasks death's lies."[48] Christ's resurrection changes how we as Christians understand death. Our loved one's death and his or her body "is a sign of remembrance and thanksgiving for all that we have received in and through this person's life and also a sign of hope that death has done its worst and lost, because the God who defeated death in the raising of Jesus Christ has also raised this child of God."[49]

QUESTIONS FOR DISCUSSION

What do you think happens after death?

What do you recall the Bible saying about what follows death?

Do you think we will be in a period of rest?

Do you think there will be a waiting period, or will we immediately be with the Lord?

Do you think our spirits actually sleep?

Awaiting Resurrection: The Time between Death and Resurrection

Physical death has occurred. We have buried our loved one. Now what? Is there time between death and resurrection, as we creatures understand time? Do we sleep or are we completely aware of our surroundings? Scripture provides us with two ways to understand what happens after death. One way is clearly seen in Luke with Jesus' words to the repentant thief dying next to Him on the cross: "Truly, I say to you, today you will be with Me in paradise" (Luke 23:43).

---

48   Long, *Accompany Them*, 46.

49   Ibid.

However you understand the term "you," whether that be the criminal's soul or his being or the "me" God created, it is clear that the repentant criminal undoubtedly was with Christ after death that very day. Paul even talks about wishing he could depart this life to be with Christ: "My desire is to depart and be with Christ, for that is far better" (Philippians 1:23). Here Paul also makes it sound as if in the very moment of death, he will be with Christ.

Yet, in his discussions with the Thessalonians, Paul also talks about death in a second way—more as if the dead will lie in state in some fashion until the Last Day, when all the saints will be gathered and raised together. "For the Lord Himself will descend from heaven with a cry of command, with the archangel's call, and with the sounds of the trumpet of God. And the dead in Christ will rise first; then we who are alive, who are left, shall be caught up together with them in the clouds to meet the Lord in the air" (1 Thessalonians 4:16–17).

So which is it? Are we immediately and wholly in union with Christ, or do we wait until the final coming of Christ to be with Him and all who have gone before us? Neither scenario perfectly provides the answer to our questions. If we are immediately and wholly in union with Christ, then the sheer reality of the dead body or box of ashes raises questions such as "If the body is here, how then are we at the same time with Christ?" Or "I see the body, I know my mom is dead, but I truly know without a doubt that my mom is wholly with Jesus." Sometimes it can be very difficult to hold these two truths together.

The first scenario highlights a more individualistic picture of eternal life, entering God's presence upon each person's death. While the second scenario removes the individualistic picture and celebrates a more general resurrection of the dead, it also turns our focus on God's victory over death, not only for the human but for the whole creation being made new. As God will ultimately bring down His "new heaven and a new earth" (a topic we will address in chapter 5), this raises many questions about where the dead are. What happens, then, as we await Christ's return? Can we be in God's presence and not yet have been resurrected? What might this look like? Let's take a look at how past theologians have tried to deal with these questions.

Thomas Aquinas[50] tried to answer these questions by attempting to fit

---

50   Thomas Aquinas was a well-known Catholic priest, Dominican friar, and doctor of the Church. He had great influence on the Church in the areas of philosophy and theology. The Catholic Church regards him as a saint and holds him up as the model teacher for those studying for the priesthood.

death into a pattern by arguing that although all persons are mortal, they are also immortal. He stated that no created being can be absolutely perishable. In Aquinas's theology, which is still visible today, he states, "It is horrible when body and soul, which were created together and will be reunited at the end times, are wrenched apart. Death is terrifying, unnatural, the worst of human evils, for the soul is the form of the body and belongs with it, and death is a violent separation of the two."[51] Aquinas clearly states that when the soul is separated from the body, a person no longer exists. This is a bit unnerving.

Similar language is often heard in the Lutheran Confessions when they speak in scriptural terms of man being composed of body and soul (see, for instance, the Epitome of the Formula of Concord, Article IX, paragraph 1; Large Catechism, Part IV, paragraph 45; and Smalcald Articles, Part III, Article I, paragraph 11). Yet, the references noted clearly teach that man's body and soul are integrally united because both are corrupted by sin and subject to death.[52] At death the soul is not annihilated, but neither does it possess immortality by virtue of natural or inherent qualities. The Athanasian Creed portrays the body-and-soul dichotomy in its teaching of Christ's two natures: "For, as the rational soul and the flesh are one human being, so God and the human being are one Christ."[53] Likewise, the Formula of Concord states, "The ancient teachers of the church have explained this union and communion of the natures using similes of a glowing iron and of the union of body and soul in the human being."[54]

Luther speaks in a similar fashion but reflects on a variety of scriptural references. In some, he reflects on the distinction of body and soul, while in others he affirms the unitary nature of man. This reflects how different Christians think differently. But biblically, there is nothing that specifically states that the body and soul are separated at death.

Other Christian theologians reject the separation of body and soul at death. Consider New Testament scholar N. T. Wright. Wright has always made a strong case to support the idea that there is one and only one resurrection of all creation. It is a future act and one that will take place when God in

---

51 Jeffrey Burton Russell, *A History of Heaven: The Singing Silence* (Princeton: Princeton University Press, 1997).

52 CTCR, *A Statement on Death*.

53 Robert Kolb and Timothy Wengert, *The Book of Concord: The Confessions of the Evangelical Lutheran Church* (Minneapolis, MN: Augsburg Fortress, 2000), p. 25, paragraph 35.

54 Ibid., p. 510, paragraph 9.

Christ re-creates all things. He is clear in stating there is no "individual pilgrimage."[55] His idea is more of a one-for-all concept, which is set at a certain time by Christ. Thomas Long questions this idea by asking, "Where then are the dead until this day?" Wright replies, "All the Christian departed are in substantially the same state, that of restful happiness."[56]

But Wright does not make clear if this means that we will be embodied when we have died and are in this restful happiness. Have all the saints already received their glorified bodies? If on one hand Wright clearly denies the platonic dualistic thought of disembodied immortal souls while on the other hand he says yes, the dead are in a blissful state embodied in restful happiness, then where are the bodies? Either way, it begins to sound similar to some sort of purgatory. If our bodies have been glorified, then what are we waiting on? If they have not been glorified, then where are they? Can they be in the ground, rotting away? This scenario leaves us with unanswered questions and in some ways provides us with a Reformed understanding of purgatory.

Although Thomas Aquinas followed a similar trajectory of body and soul separation, he was haunted by the problem of this interim state. He believed that during the interim state, the souls of the blessed were able to see God and enjoy true blessedness but were not yet able to see with a perfect vision. It was only after Christ's return that body and soul were reunited. "The perfection of the human being requires the perfection of the body."[57] Amongst the Church Fathers many assumed the idea that the soul must await the end times for a complete vision of God to come to light, while others believed and taught that God becomes immediately and wholly visible. This is the vision that still resides mainly in the Western Church. Yet, the problem of the interim state continues to frustrate theologians today. In the fourteenth century, the Catholic Church tried to answer this question for the Church by defining the interim state as a place of purgatory.

The doctrine of purgatory teaches that the souls of the just—those who have left their bodies in a state of sanctifying grace and are destined for heaven and have received a favorable judgment (albeit a conditional one)—now await

---

55   An "individual pilgrimage" means that upon death, every single person, Christian and non-Christian alike, embarks on his or her final journey to encounter either union with Christ or a separation from Christ for eternity. It is considered by most an individual personal Judgment Day.

56   Long, *Accompany Them*, 49.

57   Russell, *A History of Heaven*, 138.

a cleansing in order to appear before the presence of God. In other words, their souls contain stains of sin that have not yet been dealt with. There is no clear definition of whether purgatory is a space or place where souls are cleansed, but it is understood that purification must take place. But when can or does this happen? Unfortunately, this returns us to a state of middle ground, purgatory, or a resting period.

Although today many in the Reformed Church hold no ground with the idea of purgatory, it still resides amidst the Catholic Church. A traditional understanding of purgatory involved punishment and suffering for all involved. One did not want to stay there for any extended period of time. So, the Church constructed a way to be released from purgatory early. One could do penance, purchase indulgences, or offer up special masses to release oneself or a loved one from purgatory. This provided large sums of money for the Roman Catholic Church, but it provided little comfort for those involved, as one was never sure it was enough. This idea also leaves behind lots of questions: Once one is released, is he or she an embodied being? Is he or she 100 percent with Christ?

There is one additional teaching that Long does not discuss, and it lies mainly within Reformed theology. It is the idea of soul sleep. Luther taught and believed that the soul continues to live because it cannot be separated from God, even after the death of the body, which, he taught, decays, since it has undergone its own death at Baptism. Luther spoke of the soul "living" in peaceful sleep in his letter to Nicholas Amsdorf of 1522:

> I am inclined to agree with your opinion that the souls of the just are asleep and that they do not know where they are up to the Day of Judgment. I am drawn to this opinion by the Word of Scripture, "They sleep with their fathers." The dead who were raised by Christ and by the apostles testify to this fact, since they were as if they had just awakened from sleep and didn't know where they had been. . . . But I do not dare to affirm that this is true for all souls in general, because of the ecstasy of Paul, and the ascension of Elijah and Moses. . . . Who knows how God deals with the departed souls? Can't [God] just as well make them sleep on and off (or for as long as he wishes [them to sleep]) . . . ?[58]

---

58   To Nicholas Amsdorf (1522), LW 48:360–61. Bracketed portions added by the editors of the American Edition of *Luther's Works*.

While this theological teaching suggests that the dearly departed sleep and are unaware on the Last Day where they have been, Luther also spoke of the soul being with Christ, or in the bosom of Christ, until the Last Day, when Christ will raise all His beloved in body and soul. Paul Althaus[59] quoted Luther stating, "We are asleep until he comes and knocks on the grave and says, 'Dr. Martin, get up.' Then I will arise in a moment and will be eternally happy with him."[60]

But this raises this question: If the body has decayed, why is God returning to the grave for Luther if the soul and body have been separated? This would almost imply that the soul is with the body in the grave. Burreson in his article "The End Times in Luther: The Dear Last Day" highlights that Luther's fundamental point is not to resolve the tensions inherent in the biblical witness about the state of the soul before the Last Day because Luther also claimed that final judgment and the Last Day occurred at the moment of each individual death. "For Luther it is true that the soul both sleeps after death and experiences the Last Day immediately."[61]

The Lutheran Church—Missouri Synod, in its Commission on Theology and Church Relations document *A Statement on Death, Resurrection, and Immortality*, states:

[6.]f. [We] reject the teaching that the soul "sleeps" between death and the resurrection in such a way that it is not conscious of bliss.

7. when Scripture talks about death, the condition of the believer between death and the resurrection, and the resurrection itself, its primary purpose is to proclaim to the Christian what great things God has done for him through Jesus Christ.[62]

Long, left in the midst of theological uncertainty, admits that confusion exists about the place of our dead. He writes, "When we speak in a Christian

---

59   Paul Althaus was a German Lutheran theologian. He was appointed as associate professor of practical and systematic theology at the University of Göttingen and two years later became a full professor. He later became professor of theology at the University of Erlangen, where he welcomed the emergence of Adolf Hitler's power. Althaus lived from 1888 to 1966.

60   Paul Althaus, *The Theology of Martin Luther* (Philadelphia: Fortress Press, 1966), 415.

61   Kent Burreson, "The End Times in Luther: The Dear Last Day," 2004 Good Shepherd Institute, Concordia Theological Seminary (Fort Wayne, IN).

62   CTCR, *A Statement on Death*, observations 6f–7.

sense about death and resurrection, we are working not in clock time alone, but in at least two time frames: ordinary historical time and eschatological time (or perhaps more accurately, the eternal that transcends time)."[63]

Long provides us a way to consider numerous things happening simultaneously, things happening in human time and things happening in God's time. He describes this by considering a line drawing and being able to see the same drawing from two perceptions. Everyone, at some point, has experienced the line drawing that helps one ponder perception, the ability to become aware of something through our senses.

If you look at this line drawing you either see a candlestick or you see two faces looking toward each other; or perhaps the two images alternate for you.[64] The drawing itself hasn't changed in any way; it just provides two perceptions of the exact same image. This idea of perception, as Long suggests, allows us to consider death both from a human standpoint and from the viewpoint of God's reign, each being a different perception at the same time of the same event.

The first perception locks the human being in time and space, in the here and now. Death happens now in this time and place. Life ceases. All we can see is a dead body lying in a casket, lowered into a grave. The second perception, devoid of time and space, provides us with the view that shows our loved one surrounded by love and in the arms of Jesus.

Even Paul, as he finished his letter to the Thessalonians, stated, "and so we shall *always* be with the Lord" (1 Thessalonians 4:17, emphasis added). Even the Lutheran Confessions speak this way: "Meanwhile, because holiness has begun and is growing daily, we await the time when our flesh will be put to death, will be buried with all its uncleanliness, and will come forth gloriously and arise to complete and perfect holiness in a new, eternal life."[65]

Although Luther uses the idea of the soul being with God, he recognizes that the Christian lives with Christ, which began at one's Baptism. "It is divine truth that Abraham [after death] lives with God, serves Him, and also rules with Him. But what sort of life that is, whether he be asleep or awake,

---

63   Long, *Accompany Them*, 51.

64   Long, *Accompany Them*, 52.

65   Kolb-Wengert, *The Book of Concord*, 438.57.

that is another question. How the soul rests, we do not know; it is certain, however, that it lives."[66]

Long has made a logical argument, one that avoids dualistic thought, trying to understand where one's body is after death or the idea of purgatory. It releases the human creature from time and space and reminds us that we are to trust in God alone and put our faith in Him alone. It provides comfort and peace to those who need some sort of reassurance that we are with Christ whether in life or in death. Romans 8:38–39 reassures us of this fact: "For I am sure that neither death nor life, nor angels nor rulers, nor things present nor things to come, nor powers, nor height nor depth, nor anything else in all creation, will be able to separate us from the love of God in Christ Jesus our Lord."

Although humans living on this sinful earth may never be able to clearly define what happens to us after death, Scripture gives us glimpses into the time between death and resurrection. Jesus promises we will be in His presence:

> Truly, I say to you, today you will be with Me in paradise.
> (Luke 23:43)

Revelation 7 offers some insight as well. After seeing a vision of the Church Militant on earth being sealed with God's name to protect them amidst tribulation (vv. 1–8), John sees a vision of the Church Triumphant after the resurrection before God (vv. 9–17). These saints are standing with glorified bodies—with hands that wave palm branches, voices that sing God's praise. They no longer thirst or hunger. Their hearts no longer ache and their eyes no longer weep in mourning.

> After this I looked, and behold, [I saw] a great multitude that
> no one could number, from every nation, from all tribes and
> peoples and languages, standing before the throne and before
> the Lamb, clothed in white robes, with palm branches in their
> hands, and crying out with a loud voice, "Salvation belongs
> to our God who sits on the throne, and to the Lamb!" . . .
> Then one of the elders addressed me, saying, "Who are these,
> clothed in white robes, and from where have they come?" I
> said to him, "Sir you know." And he said to me, "These are

---

66   LW 2:216.

the ones coming out of[67] the great tribulation.[68] They have washed their robes and made them white in the blood of the Lamb. Therefore they are before the throne of God, and serve Him day and night in His temple; and He who sits on the throne will shelter them with His presence. They shall hunger no more, neither thirst anymore; the sun shall not strike them, nor any scorching heat. For the Lamb in the midst of the throne will be their shepherd, and He will guide them to springs of living water, and God will wipe away every tear from their eyes." (Revelation 7:9–10, 13–17)[69]

Conclusion

Death is an unfortunate reality we all must face. But death need not be feared. Death has been conquered; it has no hold over us. We belong to Christ. We are His, in life and in death. Our Baptism has confirmed that reality. It's a promise of the One who created us, the One who redeemed and continues to redeem us, and the One who sanctifies us. Our reality lies in the reality that Christ lived, died, is resurrected, and now lives in us. There can be no other reality, no other truth.

I tell you this, brothers: flesh and blood cannot inherit the kingdom of God, nor does the perishable inherit the imperishable. Behold! I tell you a mystery. We shall not all sleep, but we shall all be changed, in a moment, in the twinkling of an eye, at the last

---

67   "The people in the great crowd which John sees before the throne of God in heaven have already experienced 'the great tribulation' (7:14) and have come out of it. The present participle in the phrase . . . 'those who are coming out' (7:14) . . . suggests that Christians are continually emerging from this tribulation, adding to the crowd in heaven. *John is looking at the whole people of God entering and becoming the church triumphant. The crowd that John sees represents the whole church as if it were already triumphant, as if it were already complete, as it will be at the resurrection at the End.*" Louis A. Brighton, *Revelation*, Concordia Commentary (St. Louis: Concordia Publishing House, 1999), 199–200.

68   "But the church triumphant, at rest and peace and awaiting the final act of God's judgment and the resurrection at the End, will never again experience tribulation and persecution on earth." Brighton, *Revelation*, 193.

69   "Because God will tent among his saints in heaven, 'they will never again hunger nor ever again thirst' (Rev. 7:16). This description and those which follow are to be received in an eschatological, incarnational sense. The state of existence that is being described, though true now for all the saints before God's heavenly presence as 'souls' (6:9), will reach its final and full meaning *at the resurrection of the body in the new heaven and the new earth.*" Brighton, *Revelation*, 202.

trumpet. For the trumpet will sound, and the dead will be raised imperishable, and we shall be changed. For this perishable body must put on the imperishable, and this mortal body must put on immortality. When the perishable puts on the imperishable, and the mortal puts on immortality, then shall come to pass the saying that is written: "Death is swallowed up in victory." "O death, where is your victory? O death, where is your sting?" The sting of death is sin, and the power of sin is the law. But thanks be to God, who gives us the victory through our Lord Jesus Christ. (1 Corinthians 15:50–57)

No matter what happens to us after death, the promise of Christ can only bring us hope and joy because we will without a doubt be in His presence. Every need we ever had on earth is removed—no thirst, no pain, no tears. Christ becomes our all in all. What a blessing this provides. In a sense, it makes our death a moment we can look forward to with joy and excitement.

Abide with Me

1. Abide with me, fast falls the eventide.

   The darkness deepens; Lord, with me abide.

   When other helpers fail and comforts flee,

   Help of the helpless, O abide with me.

2. I need Thy presence ev'ry passing hour;

   What but Thy grace can foil the tempter's pow'r?

   Who like Thyself my guide and stay can be?

   Through cloud and sunshine, O abide with me.

3. Come not in terrors, as the King of kings,

   But kind and good, with healing in Thy wings;

   Tears for all woes, a heart for ev'ry plea.

   Come, Friend of sinners, thus abide with me.

4. Swift to its close ebbs out life's little day;

   Earth's joys grow dim, its glories pass away;

   Change and decay in all around I see;

   O Thou who changest not, abide with me.

5. I fear no foe with Thee at hand to bless;

   Ills have no weight and tears no bitterness.

   Where is death's sting? Where, grave, thy victory?

   I triumph still if Thou abide with me!

6. Hold Thou Thy cross before my closing eyes;

   Shine through the gloom, and point me to the skies.

   Heav'n's morning breaks, and earth's vain shadows flee;

   In life, in death, O Lord, abide with me.

Text: Henry F. Lyte, 1793–1847, alt. Public domain.

CHAPTER 3

FACING THE PERSONAL REALITY OF DEATH: FINDING THE "NEW NORMAL"

Introduction

> But we do not want you to be uninformed, brothers, about those who are asleep, that you may not grieve as others do who have no hope. For since we believe that Jesus died and rose again, even so, through Jesus, God will bring with Him those who have fallen asleep. For this we declare to you by a word from the Lord, that we who are alive, who are left until the coming of the Lord, will not precede those who have fallen asleep. For the Lord Himself will descend from heaven with a cry of command, with the voice of an archangel, and with the sound of the trumpet of God. And the dead in Christ will rise first. Then we who are alive, who are left, will be caught up together with them in the clouds to meet the Lord in the air, and so we will always be with the Lord. Therefore encourage one another with these words. (1 Thessalonians 4:13–18)

The pages of this chapter are filled entirely with personal experiences. These experiences are the stories of our loved ones, either through my own or someone else's intimate collision with death. Important reminder: Death is our enemy. It causes separation. God created us to live in relationship with one another. But our first and most important relationship is with our Creator. Death destroys all earthly relationships. In this life, we live in relationship with others. When we die, we are not only separated from this life, but every earthly relationship is now lost. However, there is one relationship that lasts—the one created at the baptismal font. This relationship is an everlasting relationship with God, and in this relationship there is *no* death, *no* separation, *no* brokenness.

Death causes great pain and scars us deeply. After a death occurs, we don't heal as if we suffered a disease or an illness. We never come out healed. We do come out of it, but we come out different. Different in thought, different in feeling, different in love. We are just different. Following a death, our laughter usually leaves us, at least for a while, our tears flow often, and we carry with us a deep pain that we feel can never heal. And this "different" looks different for everyone who suffers the death of a loved one.

Wherever life exists, there death also exists. Walt Wangerin, in his book *Mourning into Dancing*, says it well when he compares grief with Jesus' parable of the lost sheep. He states, "Death is one's being 'lost' to another. Cut off. Sundered. And the grief can be so deep that we rush to passionate, impractical action leaving ninety and nine in the wilderness for the sake of the one we loved."[70] The pain of grief can cripple us; it can shatter us. But it has an end. "Internally our emotions suffer the stress; our bodily functions are affected; our mental agility, our perceptions of reality, our spiritual balance all can become confused. Externally the pain affects our behavior with other people, so that those closest to us not only sense our grief but feel the pain as well."[71] A death, any death, changes who we are, and grief is the reaction to that change. "But it (grief) can accomplish a blessed rebirth in the griever."[72]

Wangerin's book provides a template that he has coined "the four acts of grief." They are used as a guide to better understand the grief that occurs after death. Normally, we hear that there are stages or steps one must take to walk through grief, meaning that we go through one stage, complete that stage, move on to the next, and so on. But when one considers grief more as an act, one in which each individual can choose to take action or not, it becomes a bit more personalized. Wangerin makes it very clear that these are simply acts of grief. They are not set rules. They are only a guide or a tool for interpreting grief. They are simply ways in which to interpret the act of grieving.[73] This is a critical statement. Grief does not hold to a set of rules to follow or steps one must take to walk though it. It is important to recognize

---

70   Walter Wangerin Jr., *Mourning into Dancing* (Grand Rapids, MI: Zondervan, 1992), 62.

71   Ibid., 150.

72   Ibid., 151.

73   Ibid., 170.

that there is no limit on the time it takes one to grieve; it lasts as long as you say it lasts. Each griever's experience is unique, and each experience leaves behind its scars. "Pain makes real this death, and this death makes real our human mortality. With pain the drama of active grieving begins. We hate this present death."[74]

Wangerin's Acts of Grief

ACT I: SHOCK

Everyone who has experienced the death of a loved one has also experienced shock. This is typically the first act of grief. At its initial onset, there are no tears, no voice, no feelings, and no cognitive thinking. We simply do not respond. It is as if we are frozen in time. In this act, we are unable to process. The body is numb to the realities that surround it. The griever chooses to feel nothing, nothing at all.

While shock may cause one person to fly into distractive activity—a continuous flow of activity that just does not stop—another may begin to experience physical diversions: pain or eruptions in the body caused by sorrow in which the body is reacting to the reality it faces without the mind truly understanding the same reality. This can be different for everyone who grieves—but it might also look different each time a person experiences grief. It seems to be true that grieving people can't express the reality of the death.

ACT II: WRESTLING WITH THE ANGEL

In this act, Wangerin reflects on Jacob's wrestling with God in Genesis 32. In the story, Jacob's fear of once again being reunited with his brother almost paralyzed him. Although he knew he needed to find peace with his brother, his fear held him back. When we are forced to deal with the death of a loved one, we, too, try to escape the pain and fear that confronts us. Jacob's wrestling with the angel reminds us of our own struggle with death. The shock caused by that death ignites fear and anger at God and at others. Yet, no matter how long and how difficult the struggle might be, we need to face death head-on. We need to trust that the Lord will walk alongside us. When we

---

74   Ibid., 198.

wrestle with the angel, we begin to transition from numbness to awakening, from shock to feeling the pain of death.

This pain is felt everywhere—not only in the body, but also in the house, the car, in every physical, spiritual, and memory experience of our loved one. Pain turns the act of grief—numbness to the death and one's being—into the drama of active grieving. Pain brings our loved one's death into reality and brings to light our human mortality. When pain surfaces, the reality of our own death hits us right between the eyes, and with this pain comes the physical struggle of wrestling with the angel. Although nothing changes, we fight and struggle, we push back, and yet, we cannot stop the death that has occurred. Our child, husband, wife, brother, sister—fill in the blank—has died and we can't do anything about it. Pain overcomes us; reality kicks in and all we can say is *nooooooooooooooooo!*

Once the pain is realized, the tears begin to flow. Feelings, all the raw feelings we left behind, now return to the body. What once was numb is now alive and flourishing with pain, extreme pain, and we can't stop it. Nobody can stop it; it flows out of us like a waterfall.

The pain sparks a flood of emotions; anger, frustration, rage, fear, even signs of denial may all begin to surface. You name it and it comes to life. All of these reactions are normal because they all are reactions that want us to believe we can control what has just happened, when in reality we have no control at all. In this act, the one grieving becomes more docile, a bit more reasonable, and in fact a bit submissive, but it is also here that one begins to rewrite the story of the loved one's death as he or she tries to create a new reality. The two big questions that arise are "What if . . . ?" and "Why?" Here we begin to try to regain the control we now realize we have lost, but in reality, never had.

ACT III: SADNESS ONLY

The struggle has come to an end and the griever looks very different to others around them. The griever has changed. Life has changed. The reality of death can be clearly seen in the griever whose spark for life has been extinguished. It is in this act, which in some ways looks very much like the first, that actions again cease, when many grievers begin to question whether life is really worth living. Sadness has taken on its own reality. There is no complexity in the mourner's mood. She or he is lonely; the heart aches. What was once a major part of one's life is now realized as being gone. Sadness is so complete that it consumes the mourner. The relationship once realized is now alive with separation and pain.

It is in this act that the griever begins to slowly die. Withdrawal from life can be seen in relationships and in activities. Grievers begin to isolate themselves from those who love and care for them. Sadness causes the griever to doubt, and he or she begins to trust no one. Reality, as the mourner once knew it, ceases to exist.

The worst manifestation of this act is withdrawal, usually withdrawal from God. God has become uncertain, unknowing, untruthful, and possibly unbelievable. God in some ways becomes the enemy rather than the comforter. In the griever's mind, especially in the Christian mind, God has caused this pain, and now we begin to question our faith and belief system. Did I ever really believe? Can I trust this God who has caused all this pain? Do I want to believe?

Reminder to those who care for the one grieving: this is normal. Every cause must have its effect. Wangerin says it this way: "The break of relationship at the beginning of grief is like lightning that splits the sky asunder; this present mortal sadness (however late it comes) is the thunder. It is death come home: this death is completing itself. . . . Don't look to the grave to find decay; look in the face of the griever."[75] A numb reality returns. There is no conversation, no daily pattern; in reality, one's entire body has begun to crumble, to slowly break apart. The world once known now begins to fall apart at each and every seam.

What can you do to help a loved one when you realize this act has come upon the griever? Hold that person tight. Talk to him or her, but don't expect conversation; just let the person hear your voice. Just be there. Walk alongside your loved one and have no expectations of anything. It will feel as if the mourner does not know you exist and may likely never remember you were there, but be there. Love the mourner through this sadness. In this way you will become for the griever the mercy of the Lord. Be there. Even today, I am not sure my sister has any recollection of the calls we shared after her daughter's death. For over a year, I called her two or three times a week. It became my daily ritual. I would pray, read Scripture, then call my little sister. Some

75   Ibid., 239.

days she felt like talking, other days she just cried, and still other days she listened while I talked. Anger still popped up its ugly head often, but I was there. I prayed that I might be a lifeline for my sister who was now dying of sadness. Whatever you do, do not try to stop this act. It is in this act that the griever for the first time is attempting to attend exclusively and honestly to the death they have experienced.

The one word that explains this act of grief is *hopelessness*. But it is in the depths of hopelessness that the psalmist says, "Out of the depths I cry to You, O LORD!" (Psalm 130:1). Here, if we listen carefully, God, who was always there, once again becomes evident by the gravity of our need.[76] In this third act we die in grief in order to experience resurrection power. Grief becomes the path we take to return to the Comforter, to return to our faith, to return to Christ who will bring new life in the midst of the death.

ACT IV: RESURRECTION

The realization comes that although death was imminent, we live. Resurrection light does not change the fact that our loved one has died, but in spite of that death, we come to realize that we are alive. Resurrection does not sweeten the bitter truth of death; it simply returns us to life and to feeling life again. It may take place very slowly, but life begins to return as a reality. "Against all reason, against all evidence—a consequence that was impossible to any who entered the Pit—you are again breathing, feeling, thinking, making decisions again."[77] We are once again alive. We are different, scarred and bruised, but we are alive nonetheless. The memory of our loved one begins to surface, it begins to provide light where only darkness once resided. And yet at the same time, life is seen with new eyes. We come to realize that life cannot be maintained by our own strength. Life is but a gift given by the Giver of life. Hopefully, the griever begins to return to the source of that life, the Creator Himself, Jesus.

This resurrection starts very slowly and progresses in minuscule movements. One day we wake up hungry and we eat. But we don't just eat; we actually taste the food, smell the spice, and enjoy the flavor. "The goodness of this moment (of the spasms of renewal) is not measured by the material thing

---

76   Ibid., 242.

77   Ibid., 273.

that caused it, but rather by the passion in you that receives it, and then by the glory of him who gives it."[78] This goodness may only last for this one moment, but life was there; it was visible. Tomorrow sadness may return, but slowly, periodically, we begin to have small moments of joy or happiness; we begin to feel and see life again. We recognize that winter has turned into spring; we feel the warm breeze that brushes our body with warmth; warmth we haven't felt in a very long time has filled us with thanksgiving. Slowly and possibly with some hesitancy, we begin to once again perform the small tasks of each day—some days with joy and others without—but we begin to trust that there just might be a future. It is a different future, yes, but a future nonetheless, a future where life exists despite—and in the midst of—death. "Death caused death. But now life reveals life and tucked within the renewal of every other relationship is proof and truth of the renewal as well as of our relationship to the Creator. . . . After grief we begin again."[79]

Each of the following stories is the personal account of a mother or a father, a sister or a brother, a wife or a husband, a daughter or a son, or a caretaker who loved someone who died very much, and how that death changed their reality.

The Death of Our Loved Ones

DEATH OF A CHILD BY STILLBIRTH OR MISCARRIAGE

Note: The term *miscarriage* is used when a baby dies before the twentieth week of pregnancy. The term *stillbirth* is used when the baby dies after the twentieth week of pregnancy or during labor or the birth itself.

Joshua Daniel was born and died on November 2, 2013. Joshua was born sleeping and died shortly before his birth while still in utero. His death even today remains a question, as the medical profession is unable to identify the cause for his parents, Kevin and Leslie. I met Kevin and Leslie when Kevin was studying for the pastoral ministry at Concordia Seminary in St. Louis. This is their story.

When the death of a child happens before he or she has actually been born,

---

78   Ibid., 275.

79   Ibid., 281–82.

people seem to think it can't hurt as much. Perhaps they think things like, "You never really got to know him." But all of this is flawed. The parents and the grandparents have spent up to nine months loving this child, investing both time and energy preparing for this child's arrival, imagining his or her life, and getting to know this child that will never be. Please, *please* don't discount the pain of the parents who lose a child before or in the process of giving birth, as in Joshua's case. Joshua was Kevin and Leslie's first child. Note the language chosen: not that Joshua *would have been* their first child. No, Joshua *was* their first child. To parents who lose a child at any age, that child is and will always be a member of their family. *Never* discount the importance of this fact.

Joshua's death came as quite a surprise. Leslie, healthy and with no problems up to that point, was ready to give birth to their first baby boy. Between the time they discovered there was something wrong until the time Joshua was pronounced dead, there were about thirty hours of prayer, begging—with Kevin pleading, "Take me instead"—and lots and lots of confusion. Kevin notes that shock flooded him at the pronouncement of the initial trouble; then, in the midst of the thirty hours, the shock dissolved, only to return with a vengeance when the doctors announced Joshua's death. But as Kevin states, because of how he died, there was still more to do—more to experience. "This was far from over for us."

As he reflects back, Kevin talks about feeling numb after his son's death. He talks about it being a time when he and his wife traded places a lot. While one of them attended to all that needed to be dealt with, the other sat numbly by, flooded by grief. Kevin vividly remembers feeling completely numb immediately following the death and recalls now how it was a defense mechanism to shield his wife from the funeral arrangements that were right around the corner.

It is still amazing how our culture seems to insist that "arrangements" for the dead need to happen immediately. There seems to be no time to process all that is and has been happening. The loss of the individual is put on the back burner, so to speak, to make arrangements for the dead in the midst of a state of numbness, which is never a good time to process anything, let alone make life-altering decisions.

Kevin continued to drift in and out of this feeling of numbness throughout the process. All of a sudden, after the funeral and for weeks after Joshua's death, a flood of depression washed over him. Today he remembers that his wife, who also had been drifting in and out of numbness, went totally numb to the realities around her so that she could care for her husband who seemed lost in depression. As Kevin has shown, this numbness, being unable to think, feel, or react normally, consumes the parent who loses a child. Their reality has been shattered by something over which they had no control. Kevin recalls how being numb allowed him to achieve certain goals, do the tasks set before him, and most importantly, tend to his wife and her emotional needs that were washing over her. Kevin recalls that although numbness helped him through some of the rougher times, it did not come without a cost. The numbness only works as a temporary protective device. The reality of the loss looms around the next corner, and it will catch up with you. Yet every so often, even today, that numbness rears its ugly head and reappears at the strangest times. There isn't a day that goes by that Leslie and Kevin don't think about Joshua. He is and will always be an intimate part of their family. Kevin reflects that feeling numb can be good, a great survival technique, but if one depends on it for too long, it begins to steal life from those who are just trying to survive.

As the numbness began to subside, the pain of Joshua's death became exceedingly evident. In many cases, as Kevin reflected back, he preferred the pain to the numbness, because only in the pain could he deal with the reality of Joshua's death. It was real, and he wanted to feel the pain of Joshua's loss; in other words, he wanted to feel Joshua. Pain is now always present in Kevin's and Leslie's lives, but they wouldn't want to change this reality, as it allows them to feel the life of Joshua and each other.

When Kevin discusses anger, especially anger toward God, he never really recalls being angry with God. He never assumed or thought God was doing this to them. He clearly remembers bargaining with God for hours upon hours during Joshua's thirty-hour struggle. He begged God to spare the life of his child and he offered himself in Joshua's place. But he also recalled that this is not how our God works, and he now has to live with what God decided that night. He still calls out to God, asking questions of clarification, and he still attempts to bargain with Him for answers, but he rests in the fact that God will make all things right and new again in His own time. Kevin states that time and distance from Joshua's death won't heal the deep wound, but it does provide perspective. As noted earlier, death changes one's reality moving forward.

For Kevin, anger was short-lived mostly because he wasn't sure who to be angry with. He felt more anger with himself because he could not protect his family from feeling all this pain. He recalls sadness being the most common and most crippling feeling of all and one that never truly goes away. For Joshua's dad, sadness makes Joshua real, and Joshua deserves to be remembered. Unfortunately, his memory carries the burden of sadness, and yet Kevin is honored to carry that sadness. But he also says he never wants this crippling sadness to leave him because if it leaves him, if he ceases to feel sadness, he ceases to remember Joshua. So, sadness becomes a part of his everyday life, a life now that recognizes Joshua's reality.

In the midst of the pain there are glimpses of what Wangerin called "resurrection." There were days when a smile would appear, but with that smile came a flood of guilt for both Kevin and Leslie. They would hear themselves say, "How can I smile when my child has died?" They ultimately came to a place where they wanted to remember Joshua with joy and not with negative feelings. Don't misunderstand: their pain is real, and it daily lives within them, but life is also real. They became pregnant again and God gave them another son. They live as changed people, people who carry pain, but people who trust in the promise of eternal life while living in this tension between life and death.

DEATH OF A CHILD

Lauren Marie was born on May 28, 1998, and died on September 22, 2001. Lauren was only three and a half. Her parents, Mary and Dave, are my sister and brother-in-law. Until the summer of 2001, Lauren was a vibrant, happy little girl who had just started preschool. There was no indication until that summer that anything at all was wrong with her health. Around midsummer, Lauren started experiencing extremely high fevers and began breaking out with a rash around her torso. Mary and Dave took her to multiple hospitals that specialize in the care of children with the same symptoms; they thought it might be juvenile arthritis. But Mary was in the midst of becoming a nurse, and she knew deep down that something else was wrong.

Mary and Dave did not find out the true answer until Lauren died and an autopsy was performed. Lauren had died of something called hemophagocytic syndrome. It is a very rare disease that primarily affects infants and young children. The latest statistics show there are only 1.2 cases per million children. Basically, this disease involves an overproduction and activation of normal infection-fighting cells. Lauren's blood cells began attacking her organs from the inside out. Even if the doctors had been able to properly diagnose Lauren, the disease had moved much too quickly to save her.

Mary and Dave deal with Lauren's death in different and significant ways. Yet, both adamantly agree that worse than their fear of losing their child is the fear of losing the memory of their child, her birthday, her favorite color, and so forth. Even today they wonder what Lauren might look like or what she might love doing, who she might have become. This year, 2018, Lauren would have been twenty.

Both Mary and Dave acknowledge that shock invaded their lives right after Lauren was pronounced dead. Dave remembers being in a "fog" for months, trying to comprehend the death of his second child and why it had to happen to them. Lauren's mother says that shock is an understatement. She remembers leaving the hospital wondering what had just happened.

Lauren had been admitted to the hospital on Tuesday of the week she died. Mary tells me that things were just not right that day; something was wrong. But by Wednesday or thereabouts, Lauren was up and about, being the typical three-year-old she was and watching *The Wizard of Oz*. Then, all of a sudden, she experienced an awful seizure, a seizure that ultimately killed her little body. Her mother, who is a nurse, says, "Lauren coded"—a medical term that means she went into cardiopulmonary arrest—"for over twenty minutes." Lauren had died. The medical team was able to resuscitate and restart Lauren's heart, but Lauren was now in a coma; her brain had been without oxygen for too long. The seizure Lauren's little body experienced had taken her life.

Lauren's motionless body lay in an unconscious state in the hospital for two or three days. As her aunts, uncles, grandmas, grandpas stopped by to see her, her parents were being asked to make the decision to remove Lauren's breathing tube, a difficult and in some ways cruel reality. Had the doctors not resuscitated Lauren, her parents would not have had to face this reality, the reality of pulling the plug on their three-year-old daughter. Although Lauren's resuscitation had provided hope, that hope was very short-lived, and now

FACING THE PERSONAL REALITY
OF DEATH—CHAPTER 3

Lauren's final heartbeat was put squarely in David and Mary's hands. It's not an easy decision for any parent.

Mary continually felt like she was trapped in a nightmare that lasted at least a year; still today sometimes it haunts her. Every morning she would get up and check Lauren's room, thinking she would be tucked away in bed, waiting for her mom to come and get her up. She could smell Lauren's scent and she knew she would be there. But every morning, as she walked into Lauren's room, that reality of her not being there hit her squarely in the face once again. She says it was worse than any nightmare she could ever experience. Dave remembers waking up and saying, "Phew! That was an awful nightmare. Now I can go back to sleep." But the nightmare couldn't go away; it was and is real. "My baby girl is gone."

Both Mary and Dave recognize the reality of numbness. For Dave, it showed up in different forms. He says it felt more like indifference and a lack of caring about so many things. His tolerance for life and for people lessened. Mary states that there is still a numb feeling to the whole event even today. The days following Lauren's death still are a blur to her, but the one thing she does remember is not wanting to enter the church. She fought the idea of walking into the service, because doing this would mean that Lauren truly had died—a reality she was not ready to face. Numbness lasted off and on for almost a year for both of them.

Dave talks about a numbness still today; it keeps him, in some ways, from enjoying the beauty of life and what it has to offer. He speaks of the examples of military personnel being killed while trying to create peace, or when innocent people are killed in mass shootings. These types of incidents take him back to the death of his daughter. But when the numbness begins to subside, it brings about the pain of reality. Pain is now a part of their reality. Mary explains it as a part of your heart being taken away, leaving a gaping hole that will always exist. Her heart will never be the same.

The question of "Why?" still vividly looms for both Mary and Dave. Mary recalls the title of the book *When Bad Things Happen to Good People*, and she contemplates why Lauren, a sweet, loving three-year-old, should die. She asks, "Why us? Why are we being called to live this nightmare?" The other looming phrase that exists for Mary and Dave is "What if?" "What if we had done this? What if we had done that? Would Lauren still have died?" Unfortunately, there are no answers to these questions, and because these questions can't be answered, Mary and Dave are left feeling anger.

They feel anger—anger with God, anger with life—because Lauren's death will always be a part of their lives. Both Mary and Dave are still openly angry with God to some degree. They can't understand why God could let something like this happen. Why would He allow the death of a precious child when there is so much hatred and death happening in the world today? And both remember bargaining with God, agreeing to trade their lives for their daughter's.

Mary felt as if God did not hear her prayers or, worse, did not respond during Lauren's struggle for life. Returning to church became an obstacle. They both returned, but it was very difficult. I remember one Christmas Eve when my sister said, "If I don't go back, I know I will never see my baby girl again." This is hope speaking. This is God working through her even in the midst of her great pain. God has promised, "You will see your daughter again." This is a hope all Christians have, a gift of grace in the midst of sorrow.

Mary and David, much like Joshua's parents, remember that it took a very long time before they could once again enjoy life or even laugh after their child had died. "You feel guilty for having these feelings," they shared. "Why should I be happy or be able to do anything without my precious child being present?" These feelings lasted a very long time for both of them. But life, a different life, returned, and now they try to stay focused on the joy Lauren brought to their lives instead of the sorrow of her death.

The loss of their child caught them completely off guard. Parents are not supposed to watch their children die. But they want others to know that there is not a right or wrong way to grieve. Everyone grieves differently. Don't let anyone ever tell you that you need to "move on" or that "things will get better." Allow yourself to grieve in your own way and in your own time. Life will return; it will go on; but you have been changed. Your life is different. Many will never know what you have gone through. "But please ask us about our Lauren, because in that way she still lives on."

FROM A SISTER'S PERSPECTIVE

Jennifer, Lauren's older sister by about two years, was almost six when

Lauren died. She and I sat down to talk about what it is like to lose a sister when you don't seem to remember too much. Jennifer took a long time to search for a word that best described her life for almost two years before and after Lauren's death. The word that she came up with was *disconnected*. Of course, she also felt isolated and very confused, which seemed to start when Lauren started showing signs of illness, but this idea of being disconnected resonated with Jennifer. That had become Jennifer's new reality. She talked about events from a physical perspective, but in reality she was very distant and disconnected. She likened it to having an out-of-body experience, although she knew she wasn't.

She obviously knew something was very wrong, but she never felt like she really knew or understood all that was happening around her. She says there is a lot she can't remember, either because her mind sought to forget, or because she just can't connect all the disconnected memories—which is probably typical for a five-and-a-half-year-old. But more than anything, she remembers people always telling her they were sorry, and she honestly didn't know what to do with that.

For the entire first year after Lauren's death, Jennifer had lots of questions, but she was afraid to ask them because she knew that just the mention of Lauren's name brought pain and sadness to her parents and other family members. She knew Lauren was gone, but she didn't completely understand all that came along with that. She vividly remembers looking for answers, but she didn't really know where to go or who to talk to. As Jennifer and I talked, she began to weep. She still has lots of emotions tied to her sister's death. Around the time she became a student in high school, she started having a lot of fear because her memories of Lauren seemed to be drifting away, and that scared her. She didn't want to lose her sister again. So now she needed to ask questions and find answers to cement the memories in her mind.

Today, Jennifer is studying to be a physician's assistant. Whether that is connected to the death of her sister, no one really knows, but Jennifer has grown up to be a loving, caring, beautiful young lady. Her memories of Lauren are alive and well, and she has been able to medically understand why Lauren died. Today, Jennifer is very attuned to and has great empathy for those who are hurting, and this is probably directly connected to Lauren's death, as she felt her parents' pain for years.

Jennifer has no idea whether she may or may not carry the gene that caused her sister's illness—it is hereditary—but she can't focus on that now. She loves life and has found some peace associated with the loss of her sister, but each year, usually through Facebook, Jennifer celebrates Lauren's birthday and the anniversary of her death by praising her little sister with amazing love. Jennifer is also keenly aware that she will one day see her little sister again.

DEATH OF A PARENT

It's interesting that I should be writing this section about my mom right now, because as I do so, it is near the anniversary of my mother's death. June Ann was born on October 1, 1931, and died January 27, 2010. She was only seventy-nine years old. She had bravely survived breast cancer only to die of colon cancer about two years later. June was the mother of six children, and at the time of her death, she had eight grandchildren. Her loving husband also died of cancer in 1998. June was full of life and loved it to the fullest. She was spunky and stood up for what was right. She loved her family dearly and missed her husband terribly.

I recall the death of my mother with vivid images. My mom was brought to the hospital about one week before her death. Her lungs had filled with fluid and needed to be drained. Most of my brothers and sisters came to the hospital within the first two days of her arrival. Our big topics of conversation in those days included lots of questions. Who would she move in with? Who would best be able to care for her? She didn't want to return home, so we all tried to figure out where she best would find rest and recovery. Unfortunately, these conversations did not last long because Mom took a turn for the worse, and we all realized she probably would not be leaving the hospital. Soon my mom was moved to another room; I guess, thinking back, it was more like a hospice room. She died there a few days later.

The call from Anne came in at 1:30 a.m. the day our mother died. I remember feeling absolutely numb. There was no doubt she was dying—I was walking through it with her—but when it actually happened, I went numb. My two other sisters and I dressed and drove to the hospital to say our final goodbyes. Around three or four o'clock in the morning, we all returned to the home where we were staying, all with very little to say. Numbness was all that we could feel. I held back the reality of all that had just happened. One moment we were talking about housing and the next we were planning her funeral. Since our mother was living in South Carolina before her death and most of her loved ones and family lived in the Midwest, her ashes had to be carried by plane to be returned home. I asked to have this honor. A funeral service was held in South Carolina while another was being planned in Wisconsin, where June spent most of her life.

I don't recall shock as much as an immense feeling of loss and emptiness. A huge part of her had been torn away from me, and a hole existed where my heart used to be. For months, maybe a year or longer, after my mother died, I had the urge to pick up the phone to call her. But then I would come to the realization that I just couldn't. My mom would never be there to answer the phone again.

The loss of a parent is different. Someone who has literally known and loved you unconditionally your entire life is suddenly no longer there, anywhere. There is no one to call when you are having a bad day or when you become ill. My mom was always there, until overnight we all became orphans. She was not only my mom but also one of my favorite people. Every year when the calendar flips over to January, the memories of my mother flood back as I anticipate remembering the day she died. I am filled with love, joy, sadness, and tears. Every year gets a bit easier, but there is always pain and sadness alongside joy and laughter. The pain of my mother's death never truly subsides; it just becomes a part of my life.

I don't recall being mad at God, because I knew without a doubt that the night my mom died, Jesus came to escort her into His presence. I recall a conversation with her a couple days before she died. She was asking, "When will He come for me? What is taking Him so long?" Of course, these were questions I couldn't answer. Recalling these questions now, I realize she was ready to be with Jesus, and this brings comfort beyond belief. My mom will always be remembered with joy and happiness. She was a bright light of joy and peace, and now she rests safely, and without pain, in the hands of her Creator.

DEATH OF A SPOUSE

My co-author's father, Allen Lowell, was born on December 25, 1936, and died at age 65 on September 26, 2002. His wife, Sue, shared his story.

Allen was a graduate of Valparaiso University and the University of Cincinnati Law School. He felt a real calling to his profession. He felt the law profession needed honest, Christian, dedicated people. He felt the Lord had called him to be that person, and that was how he carried out the mission set before him.

Allen was diagnosed with a progressive muscle disease in 1993. He had been a runner, golfer, and basketball player. Although it was a slow progression, the disease was life-changing for him. Being a man of faith, he faced each day as a challenge and with a smile. The muscle disease progressed to the point that he began using a scooter for stable mobility. Unfortunately, after returning from his law office one day, he fell backward from his scooter, hitting his head with tremendous force. The damage was so significant that surgery was not an option, and he fell into Jesus' waiting arms.

Sue does not remember feeling shock so much as feeling as if there were an immense hole deep inside her, as if someone had cut a part of her away. She recalls feeling that she and Allen truly were two people who became one perfect union. God had brought them together in this union with a total commitment to each other. When one partner is gone, the loss is devastating and leaves one traveling forward in a deep fog. She remembers how difficult it was to make decisions, and still today she does not remember a lot of the events that took place after Allen's death. But she knows without a doubt that she couldn't deny his death because she vividly felt the presence of this amazing hole in her body. That missing piece was Allen.

Instead of anger with God, Sue felt an amazing closeness to God, a closeness she admits she had never experienced before. She felt God sustaining her in the midst of her grief and literally, at times, walking right alongside her, holding her up. She also knew that Allen was no longer in pain and that he was finally at peace. And she knew without a doubt that she would see him again.

Unfortunately, sadness is now a part of Sue's life. Every new adventure, good or bad, is taken without her other half. She is sad that these are things they didn't get to share together. When she experiences new adventures, she can't help but think of Allen. Even after fifteen years, she misses him terribly. But since Allen's death, God has continued to fill her life with so many things that provide her purpose, like her children, her grandchildren, and many Christian friends. She believes it took a year or more before she was able to feel some sort of joy again in her life, but gradually that joy did return. For

Sue, some of the harder realities are having to eat meals alone and feeling as though she is a fifth wheel among her friends. But God has an amazing way of making those little difficulties become smaller and smaller over time. And He has given her the strength to seek joy in the midst of her pain.

Sue concludes her thoughts with the following paragraph, and I could not have written it any better:

> Death of a loved one is devastating! But with a strong faith, one can move beyond it and have a fulfilling life. It will just be a different life. I used to tell Allen I wanted to grow old with him. Now I must do that alone, but I also know, one day, I will be with him again in the presence of our heavenly Father. I don't know how anyone makes it through this grief process without faith. . . . You face each day one at a time and eventually a new life opens up. I can't stress enough the importance of keeping a close relationship with God and praying for strength and guidance each moment!

Revelation 14:13 has been an important word of God that has sustained her faith in the Lord who will raise Allen on the Last Day: "And I heard a voice from heaven saying, 'Write this: Blessed are the dead who die in the Lord from now on.' 'Blessed indeed,' says the Spirit, 'that they may rest from their labors, for their deeds follow them!'"

DEATH BY SUICIDE

I have known Mimi and Mike almost my whole life. They had nine children and our family had six. Our families practically grew up together. This is the story of their son Paul Gerard, who was born January 18, 1968, and died May 4, 1986. Paul's death at age 18 was a watershed event for his entire family because Paul committed suicide.

Mimi states that it is hard to tell the story of Paul's death without first understanding the death of her sister Margaret, who also died at age 18, on June 5, 1956. Margaret died in a car accident while she was taking her grandmother's nurse home. Mimi recalls how very angry she was with God that day. "Why would God choose to take such a good and holy person?" Mimi was only twenty-four at the time and had never had to deal with grief. It was a raw and very new experience. She goes on: "I was about to get married in two months, and Margaret was to be my bridesmaid." In 1956, after Margaret's funeral, as Mimi sat weeping in a church pew, a local priest shared with her the story of his sister and husband who died on their honeymoon in a similar way to her sister.

Mimi recalls how, in the days following Margaret's death, she prayed for a sign from God that Margaret was at peace. One day while off with her mother and friends, making plans for her upcoming August wedding, she and her family were called to her grandmother's bedside. Only a month after Margaret's death, their grandmother now lay dying. Mimi, her sister, and mother rushed to her bedside. They made it just in time to say goodbye. Now her grandmother had also died, and once again, grief flooded her heart. Yet, later in the day, the doorbell rang, and she went to answer it. As she opened the door, there stood a woman with a handful of flowers—not just any flowers, but a bouquet of white roses. The woman stated, "These are for you." In the midst of her sorrow, Mimi quickly came to the conclusion that these flowers were an answer to her prayer, the sign she needed that Margaret was with Jesus. With this amazing gift, Mimi began to heal. The following day, her fear, anger, and frustration began to subside, for she knew she now needed to allow the healing process to begin. Margaret was with God, and her goodness had come from her faith in God.

This background story of Margaret's death at eighteen gives us insight into Paul's mom's story of death, anger with God, grief, pain, and the power to overcome all and lean on God. Margaret's death provided Mimi with the grace and strength she would need to deal with her own son's death.

Fast-forward thirty years to the day Paul died. His parents, Mike and Mimi, were visiting friends in Kentucky when they got the call that Paul had died. On the flight back home to Wisconsin, Mimi kept repeating, "Come Lord Jesus, come." When they were originally notified of his death, they had no idea that he had committed suicide. This was only discovered as they inched closer to home. Mimi vividly remembers walking in the front door only to find their sixteen-year-old son, Christopher, sitting alone on the couch. He was pale, numb, and in shock. Only hours earlier, Christopher had found Paul's body hanging in their basement. This vision is and will always be a very painful memory for her. Numbness, fear, and pain flooded over both Paul's parents.

But Paul was one of twelve children, three whom had died previously in

miscarriages. So Mike and Mimi had their hands full with eight other children. They remember saying to each other, "We have to find a balance." So they turned to the one thing they could trust: their faith. As difficult and painful as it was for them, whenever the "why" question reared its head, Mike kept repeating, "There are no answers. We just need to trust." Paul's final words left in a note said, "Forgive me for I know not what I do."

Mimi knows without a doubt that her daily participation in the Mass is what provided her the strength she needed to walk through this awful experience. It was a journey of faith and trust. It allowed her to be there and serve her family in the midst of her grief. It gave her the strength to get out of bed every morning, to walk with an open heart and spirit, and to allow God to do His work through her. It is by God's grace alone that she now provides grace and joy to others.

Mike and Mimi decided the family should attend counseling as a group. Unfortunately, this was a huge bust. Whether because it was the wrong counselor, or because it was too early in the process, Mike and Mimi will never know, but both promised all their children that if they needed any help at all, they would provide it. For years following Paul's death, his parents spent time talking to the local schools about suicide and its effects on the family. They admitted they knew nothing more about suicide except the pain and grappling with the grief that floods the entire family and community. Paul's death allowed them to talk and listen to others in similar circumstances. All of this helped them walk through this tragedy, along with the daily reading of Psalm 118:24: "This is the day the LORD has made; let us rejoice and be glad in it."

DEATH VIA A TERMINAL DISEASE

This is the story of Michael Wayne, who was born December 29, 1942, and died September 24, 2004. Michael and his wife, Carla, were close Christian friends of mine when I lived in California.

Michael was an avid race car driver who was diagnosed with pancreatic cancer at age 62. Mike, as his friends and family knew him, continued to race until one month before his death. The week before Mike died, the speedway where Mike's career began held a tribute race commemorating Mike's forty-year career. At this point in Mike's fight with cancer, his body was too weak to drive the race car, but he was able to attend the race that evening. Another driver drove the car that Mike had designed and built with his own two hands, and that evening his car won the main event. It was a bittersweet tribute to a life well lived.

Carla admits that at age 58, she had never experienced a death that would impact the rest of her life until her beloved Mike died. She remembers the road, if you will, to Mike's final breath. Mike was a man of God and was completely content whether he lived or died. For Mike, it was a win-win situation. If he lived, he would be blessed to spend more time with his wife, and if he died, he would be with Jesus. Mike looked forward to being with Jesus. Whichever way the pendulum swung, Mike was totally at peace. This provided peace for Carla too. Since there was no fear of death, Mike and Carla chose not to live in darkness during his illness; instead, the curtains were wide open each day, and there was an open invitation for any and all to come and spend time with Mike.

One day as Mike's pastor was visiting, Mike asked him, "So what are you going to say at my funeral, Pastor?" His pastor smiled at Mike and said, "I haven't gotten that far yet, Mike. Be patient with me." Then Mike went on to say, "Okay, but I will be bringing you a flock on that day, so be prepared to shepherd them. They need to hear God's amazing grace." Some people who first encountered God's amazing grace at Mike's funeral still attend that church to this day.

On another day, not long before Mike died, he was saddened at the thought of never being able to see it rain again once he died. With no forecast of rain in the near future, family and friends prayed for rain so that Mike might be able to see and feel it rain one last time. Then, one amazing Sunday—in fact, his last Sunday on God's earth and the first Sunday he was too weak to attend church—with the sun shining brightly, someone noticed it was beginning to get dark outside. The clouds rolled in, the sky became dark, heavens opened up wide, and rain, beautiful rain, poured from the heavens above. Some were heard saying, "Look, Mike's rain!" Many who had prayed for rain heard later that Mike, with the help of his wife, moved outdoors to be soaked by this beautiful rain. Mike felt blessed and loved by God.

Carla reflects that one of the hardest things Mike had to do was call friends and relatives to tell them he was only going to be with them a short time longer. His mother took the news the hardest because she still blamed God for Mike's father's tragic death at only twenty-nine years old. Mike talked to his mother almost daily, sharing his faith and love for Jesus. Slowly her anger faded, and she was able to finally hear Mike's words and feel Jesus' love. She came to Mike's memorial service and sat in the front row, listening intently to the pastor's words. After the service, she told me that she was finally at peace and could submit to God's decision and accept His grace. Two years later she joined Mike in paradise.

Because Mike was so prepared for his death and had no fear of dying, his wife was at peace most of the time. She was never really angry with God, but she does remember bargaining with Him: "If the cup could be taken away from Mike, then I will promise this, or I will promise that." After Mike's death, Carla remembers a feeling of numbness, and looking back, she realized she had made many life-altering decisions she never would have agreed to had she not been numb. She remembers a feeling of panic that his death couldn't be changed and she would now need to live the rest of her life without Mike. A deep sadness flooded her. She would tell herself and others she was fine and in control, but in reality she was out of control and actually could not handle this loss by herself. She needed to lean on Jesus. Although Mike was gone, Jesus wasn't. She would find a new strength and a new love for life in the people God was putting in her life to help and comfort her.

Although Carla accepts Mike's death, she still dreams about him almost every night. Unfortunately, some of the dreams turn out more like nightmares, and these scare her at times, but this is when she turns herself back over to God's care and trusts in Him alone. Mike's death has changed the life Carla now lives. Her faith is stronger, her joy is deeper, her love and compassion for others has deepened her relationships, and today she walks with others as they walk closer to death. When Carla was told that she had stage 3 breast cancer, her thoughts turned to Mike's Christian faith: "Whatever the outcome, it's a win-win. I either continue to live or I die and get to be with Jesus." As Mike's final days drew near, Carla remembers, Mike lost all care for the material things of this world and instead looked forward to being with Jesus. Carla even today prays for that courage and strength.

Carla knows without a doubt that today she is not the same person she was before Mike's death—she is actually a better person and more attuned to other people's needs. For this she is thankful.

DEATH OF A PET

Although we do not all experience the loss of a pet in the same way as we do a spouse, child, or other loved ones, many people have shared that the experience of losing a family pet is also tragic and painful.

This is the story of Pugs. Pugs was the first of many pets Bill and Traci were blessed to have as part of their family. Pugs was adopted from the Humane Society, a place many go to find a furry friend to love. Pugs shared thirteen years with her new family. She was a fast runner, an extraordinary hole digger, a cute beggar of food, a comedian, a sun adorer, a momma to a newly adopted kitten, and a friend and protector to the other dogs and cats in her life. She was a treasure to her family and brought joy to all she met.

As Pugs aged, she struggled with dementia. Although this changed many things in her life, she continued to be a joy and a beloved member of her family. Eventually, they sadly knew the time was coming to relieve Pugs of her struggles and let her be at peace. They prayed for God's guidance for the right time and for peace in the ultimate decision. The days and weeks leading up to this final decision were agonizing and heartbreaking, as Pugs had brought them all such great joy. When the day finally arrived, there was deep heartache and sadness. Pugs was held and comforted, and she was not alone. Pugs was in their arms when her life drifted away, but they feel like she is still with them in spirit. A quote by an unknown author seems appropriate for Pugs and perhaps others: "Some fears and eccentricities will lift with the years; others will only deepen. One by one, the things you love to do become too difficult and slip out of your life. But despite it all, you will still be you, and people will cherish your wobbly presence. Even a diminished life is worth living on its own terms."

The death of a pet in most cases is different because the people who love their pet are often asked to make a vital decision on when the death occurs, unlike the death of a spouse, child, or parent over which we have no control. This is a huge decision, but many who care for pets are faced with this dilemma at one time or another. As Traci explained, the decision-making is the worst part about loving an animal. Struggling with fears and yet wanting to do the right thing for the pet are so difficult. But once a decision has been made, most feel at peace and are able to rejoice and be very thankful for the time they were given. Even now, twenty-three years later, memories of Pugs flood her family's hearts and minds. They think of Pugs with joy and remember her special qualities. Pugs was very special, the first of six dogs and nine cats this couple would have in their lives. Each pet has brought them joy in a life well lived and sadness when they died. Each was a special gift created by God to be loved. God cares for all that He created. Bill and Traci take comfort in knowing without a doubt that Pugs was and is loved by God. Her memory continues in the hearts of those who loved her.

Although the death of a pet is different, it does not lessen the loss or the pain of death. Pets play a huge role in the family, and the people who love their pets want others to know that the death of a pet is painful. As heart-wrenching as a pet's death is, having that pet in our lives brings so much happiness and love that it overshadows the pain and sadness. Each pet is unique; each one's life matters. Pugs was unique, and her life mattered.

*Things **Not** to Say to Someone Who Is Grieving*

LOSS OF A CHILD THROUGH MISCARRIAGE OR STILLBIRTH

"Thank God you didn't actually get to know him/her. If you had, this would have been completely unbearable." The problem with this statement is that the parents *have* gotten to know their baby. The mother has carried their child in her belly. The baby was a part of the family.

"At least there wasn't actually a baby." But there was a baby! Those that defend abortion are totally comfortable in stating this was not a child, but it gives no credence to the fact that God calls it a child.

"Don't worry; you can have another child." But the reality is you can never have *that* child. This child has died. There is no such thing as a replacement child.

"It just wasn't meant to be." No one, and I mean no one, knows this for a fact. This is plainly a cold and callous statement.

"It was for the best." "It's nature's way of getting rid of a mistake." A mistake? Really? Remember, God doesn't make mistakes. Only humans do.

FOR ANY LOSS

"Things happen for a reason." Of course they do, but this brings no comfort to the one dealing with the loss. In a sense, this statement is someone trying to play God.

"God needed your loved one more than you did." Where does one find comfort in this statement? It turns God into a vicious and vengeful God who gives only to take away.

"What can we do to help?" This puts the burden on the one mourning. A better way to handle it might be to say, "You might not feel like talking right now, but I will be in the lobby, the living room, wherever if you need a hug." This now becomes an open invitation.

"It will all be okay." No, it actually won't *ever* be okay while we live on this earth. But the goal here is to look toward the resurrection. When it occurs, we will be gathered together with our loved ones who have gone before us, and we will rejoice as one with our God.

"It is God's will." This is a huge assumption on our part and very easy to misunderstand. If a loved one was murdered, it would be monstrous to imply it was God's will.

"God never gives us more than we can handle." People always say this is from the Bible, but it is not. Here is the text many use as the basis for this statement: "No temptation has overtaken you that is not common to man. God is faithful, and He will not let you be tempted beyond your ability, but with the temptation He will also provide the way of escape, that you may be able to endure it" (1 Corinthians 10:13). This text is about temptation. God will never allow us to be tempted beyond our ability. Of course, if you consider grief as a temptation to doubt God, then maybe this passage applies, but that is not its intent.

QUESTIONS FOR DISCUSSION

How has someone's death affected your life? How might it have changed you?

If you have lost a loved one, what can you share with others that might provide them the strength and courage to trust God's promise alone?

If you have experienced mourning in a different way that hasn't been identified elsewhere in this chapter, consider sharing it with others.

How might what you have read in this chapter provide guidance and direction to those you might walk with in the future as they mourn?

If you are comfortable doing so, share the loss of someone you loved.

If you have lost someone you love, how has looking forward to the resurrection changed or altered your grief?

Luther's Word of Comfort to Those Who Grieve

It is true that a Christian in deepest despair does not dare to name, wish, or hope for the help (as it seems to him) which he would wholeheartedly and gladly purchase with his own life were that possible, and in doing so thus find comfort. However, the words of Paul, Romans 8 [:26–27], properly apply here: "Likewise the Spirit helps us in our weakness; for we do not know how to pray as we ought (that is, as was said above, we dare not express our wishes), rather the Spirit himself intercedes for us mightily with sighs too deep for words. And he who searches the heart knows what is the mind of the Spirit," etc. Also Ephesians 3 [:20], "Now to him who by the power at work within us is able to do far more abundantly than all that we ask or think."[80]

What Those Who Are Grieving Want You to Know

Death changes the reality of those who are forced to deal with it. Many times, you can't see the pain and sorrow in those who live in the midst of it, but it is there right below the surface. Don't forget about us; we need you. We need your love and your support for the rest of our lives. Come to us, because we probably can't or won't come to you. Think of us often, and keep us in your prayers.

---

80   Martin Luther, "Comfort for Women Who Have Had a Miscarriage," WA 43:247–50.

Usually, once a funeral has taken place, people return to their daily routine, but our routine has changed forever; it will never be the same. Help us by letting us know you still remember. Just be there; talk with us about our loved ones. Yes, it hurts, but knowing you still remember helps us.

Our Help Comes from the Lord

Our help, our hope, our love and trust all come from the Lord. Jesus walks with us in the midst of all our suffering, in our deep and painful despair. He hears the silent cry of our hearts. He loves us more than any human being could love, and He points us all toward His bodily resurrection and eternal life with Him. In His resurrection He clearly states our victory and the victory of all Christians—our own bodily resurrection.

This Body in the Grave We Lay

1. This body in the grave we lay
   There to await that solemn day
   When God Himself shall bid it rise
   To mount triumphant to the skies.

2. And so to earth we now entrust
   What came from dust and turns to dust
   And from the dust shall rise that day
   In glorious triumph o'er decay.

3. The soul forever lives with God,
   Who freely hath His grace bestowed
   And through His Son redeemed it here
   From ev'ry sin, from ev'ry fear.

4. All trials and all griefs are past,
   A blessed end has come at last.
   Christ's yoke was borne with ready will;
   Who dieth thus is living still.

5. We have no cause to mourn or weep;
   Securely shall this body sleep
   Till Christ Himself shall death destroy
   And raise the blessed dead to joy.

6. Then let us leave this place of rest
   And homeward turn, for they are blest
   Who heed God's warning and prepare
   Lest death should find them unaware.

7. So help us, Jesus, ground of faith;
   Thou hast redeemed us by Thy death
   From endless death and set us free.
   We laud and praise and worship Thee.

Text: Michael Weisse, ca. 1480–1534, sts. 1–6; *Gesangbuch*, Magdeburg, 1540, st. 7; tr. William M. Czamanske, 1873–1964. Public domain.

CHAPTER 4

YOUR VICTORY— THE BODY'S RESURRECTION

Introduction

I tell you this, brothers: flesh and blood cannot inherit the kingdom of God, nor does the perishable inherit the imperishable. Behold! I tell you a mystery. We shall not all sleep, but we shall all be changed, in a moment, in the twinkling of an eye, at the last trumpet. For the trumpet will sound, and the dead will be raised imperishable, and we shall be changed. For this perishable body must put on the imperishable, and this mortal body must put on immortality. When the perishable puts on the imperishable, and the mortal puts on immortality, then shall come to pass the saying that is written, "Death is swallowed up in victory." "O death, where is your victory? O death, where is your sting?" The sting of death is sin, and the power of sin is the law. But thanks be to God, who gives us the victory through our Lord Jesus Christ. (1 Corinthians 15:50–57)

In this way, Paul concludes his confession of the resurrection that is 1 Corinthians 15. Paul's entire point in the chapter is that those who believe the Gospel message place their trust and hope in the Messiah, Lord Jesus, who is victorious over the great enemy, death, and everything associated with death. Jesus' victory over death through His own death and resurrection is, for those whose faith is in Jesus, their victory over death. In Christ we are victorious in all ways. Chrysostom, the great fifth-century preacher, put it this way:

Seest thou his noble soul? how even as one who is offering sacrifices for victory, having become inspired and seeing already things future as things past, he leaps and tramples upon death fallen at his feet, and shouts a cry of triumph over its head where it lies, exclaiming mightily and saying, "O death, where is thy sting? O grave, where is thy victory?" It is clean gone, it is perished, it is utterly vanished away, and in vain hast thou done all those former things. For He not only disarmed death and vanquished it, but even destroyed it, and made it quite cease from being.[81]

Christians live within the confession of this truth: we have conquered death! That victory of Christ shapes our living in this life. We can face death and walk through the valley of death with confidence because death has no sting. We can also enter into our ongoing dying in this life and the moment of our death as an act of bold confession, trust, and hope because this life has no permanency but the life to come does. We can die to this life because we will live in Christ. As Paul says in Romans 14:8–9, "If we live, we live to the Lord, and if we die, we die to the Lord. So then, whether we live or whether we die, we are the Lord's. For to this end Christ died and lived again, that He might be Lord both of the dead and of the living." Christ lives eternally and so shall we. His resurrection victory is our resurrection victory!

Victory over Death: Christ Jesus' Bodily Resurrection

There is only one who has conquered death: Christ Jesus the Lord! Apart from Him there can be no victory over death and its consequences. His victory over death is a bodily victory. It is not some ghost or specter or spiritual being that God raises from the dead (1 Corinthians 6:14). God raised Jesus' body from the dead (Romans 10:9), His physical body that was born of His blessed mother, the Virgin Mary. The disciples saw this raised Jesus in His flesh, as Paul recounts in 1 Corinthians 15:3–8:

> For I delivered to you as of first importance what I also received:
> that Christ died for our sins in accordance with the Scriptures, that
> He was buried, that He was raised on the third day in accordance
> with the Scriptures, and that He appeared to Cephas, then to the
> twelve. Then He appeared to more than five hundred brothers at
> one time, most of whom are still alive, though some have fallen

---

81   John Chrysostom, *Homilies on the Epistles of Paul to the Corinthians* in P. Schaff, et. al., eds., *A Select Library of the Nicene and Post-Nicene Fathers of the Christian Church*, series 1, vol. 12 (New York: Christian Literature, 1887–94; reprint: Peabody, MA: Hendrickson, 1994), 257.

asleep. Then He appeared to James, then to all the apostles. Last
of all, as to one untimely born, He appeared also to me.

When Jesus appeared to the Twelve the first time, Thomas was not with them.
But a week later Jesus appeared a second time and Thomas was with them.
After placing his fingers into the wounds in Jesus' hands and placing his hand
into the spear wound in His side, Thomas confessed Jesus as his Lord and
his God (John 20:26–28). Jesus' victory over death is a bodily victory. In His
resurrection, death no longer had the power to destroy His earthly body. Jesus
will live forever in the body that was born of Mary.

Jesus' resurrected body was indeed the same body that was His before His
death, but it was also transformed, or transfigured. He already had given a
foretaste of this transformation before His death through His transfiguration
(see Matthew 17:1–8; Mark 9:2–8; Luke 9:28–36). There His body glowed
with the glory that belongs to Him as the Son of God, His divinity fully shining forth in His person and shared with His humanity. After His resurrection,
this transformation became permanent. God thoroughly perfected and glorified His body.

The transformation was so thorough that initially the disciples were not
able to or were kept from recognizing Him (see John 20:14; 21:4; Luke 24:16;
24:37). Eventually, through His words and by faith, they saw Him clearly as
the glorified Jesus. It certainly was no ordinary body that belonged to Him.
He was not limited by space or time (passing through a sealed tomb and closed
doors), appearing wherever He desired whenever He desired. Right now we
can only know through a glass darkly what His postresurrection transfiguration meant for His body. We have never seen a body glorified and perfected by
God. All we have to go on are the accounts of these eyewitnesses.

Mysteriously, Jesus' postresurrection body is the same one that walked the
earth before His gruesome death. And yet, it was different, as the disciples saw
by faith. In His resurrection, Jesus revealed His glorified body. Here was the
person of the Crucified One, now risen, the holy and glorified Jesus. He fully
revealed the transformation of the human person that comes from the union
of the Son of God with the Son of Man in the incarnation and now eternally
established in His resurrected body.

This risen Jesus, completely in the glorified flesh, will come again on the earth. Matthew says, "When the Son of Man comes in His glory, and all the angels with Him, then He will sit on His glorious throne" (Matthew 25:31). Matthew's use of the term "Son of Man" highlights that the ruling one who returns is the Jesus who was very much human, in the flesh. Everyone will physically see Him in the glory of His Father. Jesus in the flesh will return as the almighty ruling one (Acts 1:11).

QUESTIONS FOR DISCUSSION

Why is it important to confess Jesus' bodily resurrection?

When we confess Jesus' bodily resurrection we are simply saying that He is truly God in the flesh, the Word of God incarnate, who by His death and resurrection, by His Passover from life to death at the hands of sinful people, conquered death, sin, evil, the devil, and hell. His bodily resurrection means that all of creation participates in the Creator's victory over all those forces.

What does Jesus' resurrection tell us about our future?

Paul says it best in 1 Corinthians 15:17–19: "And if Christ has not been raised, your faith is futile and you are still in your sins. Then those also who have fallen asleep in Christ have perished. If in Christ we have hope in this life only, we are of all people most to be pitied." Jesus' resurrection means that those who have died in Jesus will be raised bodily and will enter into His eternal rule and reign.

The Last Great Enemy: Death

If Jesus is the one who will be enthroned as the almighty ruling one, then all things must be put into subjection under His feet (1 Corinthians 15:27). As Paul acknowledges, the last thing to be put into subjection under His feet—to be destroyed—is death (v. 26), the last great enemy. And it *is* an enemy. It is not according to God's will. It is not natural or normal. It is not a part of life; it is opposed to life. This is why Jesus wept at the grave of Lazarus (John 11:35).[82] Death is the great enemy of bodily life and of the author of life, the living God.

---

82   Alexander Schmemann, *O Death, Where Is Thy Sting?* (Yonkers, NY: St. Vladimir's Seminary Press, 2003) 30–32.

When physical death entered the creation as a consequence of our sin through Adam and Eve, it grabbed hold of the entire universe and permeated all things, physical and spiritual. Death's presence is pervasive. Death manifests itself physically when our heart stops beating, our lungs stop filling with air, and our mind stops functioning.

Yet, even more insidiously, death manifests itself spiritually. Spiritual death is the wall of separation constructed between God, the source of life, and human beings. It is an impregnable wall that we erected through our sin. We have no access to God through our spirit or in our body. As Paul writes in Ephesians 2:1–3, "You were dead in the trespasses and sins in which you once walked, following the course of this world, following the prince of the power of the air, the spirit that is now at work in the sons of disobedience—among whom we all once lived."

Spiritual death, culminating in physical death, leads to the final and irrevocable form of death: eternal death. As Paul confesses in Romans 6:23, "For the wages of sin is death, but the free gift of God is eternal life in Christ Jesus our Lord." The wages of sin is spiritual death, physical death, and eternal separation from the living God: eternal death. Because it is eternal separation from God, the very source of human life, it is easy to conceive of death as the last great enemy. C. S. Lewis in *The Great Divorce* describes eternal death as an ongoing turning in toward the self, away from others and the life of God. It is narcissism run amok. As the eternally dead turn more and more inward toward themselves, they drive themselves farther and farther from God as the source of life. It is a harrowing picture. With eternal death in view, we can only cry with St. Paul, "Wretched man that I am! Who will deliver me from this body of death?" (Romans 7:24).

QUESTIONS FOR DISCUSSION

How does Jesus' death and resurrection show us that death is the last great enemy?

Physical, spiritual, and eternal death separates sinners from the living God. Only God can destroy that chasm. When Jesus entered into death through His crucifixion and emerged living on the other side of death, He showed us that the final thing that needed to be conquered is that great separation point, death, in order for us to have access to the living God.

Who brings death into the world?

While death is a punishment for sin enacted by God, death doesn't enter the world apart from human sin and the Law that exposes that sin. Paul indicates this in Romans 5:12–14: "Therefore, just as sin came into the world through one man, and death through sin, and so death spread to all men because all sinned—for sin indeed was in the world before the law was given, but sin is not counted where there is no law. Yet death reigned from Adam to Moses, even over those whose sinning was not like the transgression of Adam, who was a type of the one who was to come." We, sinful humans, bring death into the world.

What kind of death is most dangerous?

While spiritual death and physical death are frightening and dangerous in themselves, eternal death is the most dangerous and threatening because eternal death is separation from the living God, Father, Son, and Holy Spirit, for eternity. It means to "live," in whatever way that is possible, apart from the source of life itself. It is to live while dying eternally.

The Reality of Death

"Dust you are and to dust you shall return." Many Lutherans and Protestants in the twentieth and twenty-first centuries are familiar with this phrase. These words are usually spoken at the imposition of ashes in the shape of a cross on the foreheads of those who attend an Ash Wednesday service.

Ashes are a rich symbol, rooted in biblical practice, and they symbolize many things. They evoke a sense of God's judgment and condemnation of sin. They point to the frailty of human life. The ashes also confront us with the reality of death in a death-denying culture. We are reminded forcefully of the words of the committal of the dead in the burial service: "earth to earth, ashes to ashes, dust to dust." One day those words will be said over *us*. The ashes help us to remember that death always has us surrounded. There is no escaping it.

Such a ritual is especially helpfully in a society that seeks to deny the reality of death. Modern society yearns for a way to escape death or overcome it. Whether it is through the science of medicine (i.e., genetic engineering) or technological advances (i.e., transhumanism), people yearn for a way to cheat death. In the meantime, we cover death up as much as possible.

We rarely encounter the reality of death until the last minute: in the hours or days before someone dies; in the funeral home, if the body is made available for viewing; perhaps at the graveside. Beyond that, society seeks to keep death as distant as possible. The aging and dying processes are kept out of sight in retirement homes, nursing homes, institutions, and hospitals. We often don't have contact with our aging and dying loved ones on a daily basis.

At the time of death, we make the dead look as much as possible like they are still living. We embalm their bodies, doctor up their appearance, close the casket, or destroy the evidence of death through cremation. We have engineered a thorough process for hiding death as deeply underground as possible (pun intended!).

Yet, death will not so readily oblige our efforts. Our efforts at hiding death disclose its inescapability. As Schmemann notes, "Why has [death] become so powerful that the world itself has become a kind of cosmic cemetery, a place where a collection of people condemned to death live either in fear or terror, or in their efforts to forget about death find themselves rushing around one great big burial plot?"[83] Have you ever thought about the earth as one great big burial plot? Elsewhere Schmemann refers to it as a "globe stuffed with corpses."[84]

So, while we might try to escape death or at least imprison it temporarily, it will eventually escape and claim us. We watch a show on television or the news and death is everywhere, although always someone else's death. We receive a medical diagnosis that could portend death. Our parents show increased signs of age that we know will lead to death. Our loved one dies. We begin to contemplate the inevitability of our own dying. It is then that we are forced to come to grips with "a globe stuffed with corpses."

Why this endless effort to conquer death and isolate its presence? In the end it is because we sinful humans can make no sense out of death. It is meaningless. Death entails nonexistence, the loss of life and personhood, the end

83   Ibid., 32.

84   Ibid., 83.

to the trajectory of our life and of personal meaning and social significance. Death seems to give a final and completely hopeless answer to the question, Why does anyone live in this torturous and short life? Death ends any hope of making sense of the meaning of life in society's eyes.

Thus, for modern culture, death has no meaning, no potential for being a meaningful event. Death is simply a problem to be addressed. That is why we seek "solutions" to death through the medical machine and through making the experience of death as therapeutically pleasing as possible. The hospital becomes our church and home when we are confronted with death. We simply assume that the place for dying is the hospital and the people for attending to the dying are doctors, nurses, hospital aides, and social workers. And the goal for the dying and those who love them is to make sure everyone feels good.

The goal is to suppress any negative experiences that issue from the experience of death. As long as the "problem" of death is handled properly, then we will have accomplished what we intended to accomplish. If we can walk through the experience of death in such a way that it appears as harmless as possible, then we have encountered it in the way we think is best. Essentially the therapeutic way in which we approach death should lead us to be able to ignore it as much as possible. Death is cordoned off as applying only to the dead and in no way impinging upon the living.

The irony in this dead-end pursuit (pun intended again!) is that we willingly subjected ourselves to death. We pursued death when we desired to possess life for ourselves and in ourselves. In the great rebellion in the Garden of Eden, we decided that we could generate life for ourselves:

> [The serpent] said to the woman, "Did God actually say, 'You
> shall not eat of any tree in the garden'?" And the woman said to the
> serpent, "We may eat of the fruit of the trees in the garden, but God
> said, 'You shall not eat of the fruit of the tree that is in the midst of
> the garden, neither shall you touch it, lest you die.'" But the serpent
> said to the woman, "You will not surely die. For God knows that
> when you eat of it your eyes will be opened, and you will be like God,
> knowing good and evil." So when the woman saw that the tree was
> good for food, and that it was a delight to the eyes, and that the tree
> was to be desired to make one wise, she took of its fruit and ate, and

she also gave some to her husband who was with her, and he ate.
(Genesis 3:1–6)

God is life, and communion with God brings life, and God as the only truly living one brings all created things into life; therefore, succumbing to the temptation to be like God and know good and evil is to pursue being god oneself and to seek the source of one's life in oneself, apart from the living God. In doing so we denied God as life, as the source of life, and immediately fell into communion with death. We made ourselves subject to death itself.

As a result, every living thing on earth no longer was life-giving in its living, but had to die in order to give humans life. (Imagine eating plants that didn't have to die in order to be eaten but were continually renewed.) Death now was at the center of everything. Even the food we eat in order that we might live must die first in order to give us life. And the food we eat ultimately can't give us life permanently. We continue dying even as we eat. We eat death in order to live. There is no escaping it. Even as we live we are in constant communion with death.[85]

We can't escape death. And while we cannot ourselves make sense of death or twist any meaning out of death, we dare not embrace death either as something normal and natural. Death is never desirable or normal. It is always a denial of God and God's life. It is separation from God, the darkness of being isolated from God as the source of life and from our fellow living creatures. That is why Jesus wept at Lazarus's grave (John 11:35). He grieved at the separation of from life and from God that occurred with the death of His friend Lazarus, who was one of the creatures whose life was dependent upon the Word, Jesus Himself. There is no deeper meaning or purpose to be found in Lazarus's death.

Only when we realize that death is the last great enemy with whom we have thrust ourselves into communion; only when we realize that we can never tame death, pacify it, or make it our friend—only then is the door open for God to make death meaningful. Only God can transform something utterly meaningless into something meaningful. In fact, He transforms death into its very opposite—life.

---

85   I am indebted to Alexander Schmemann for this line of thought relative to communion with death through our eating. See *O Death, Where Is Thy Sting?*, pp. 32–36, 74–76.

For the trumpet will sound, and the dead will be raised imperishable, and we shall be changed. For this perishable body must put on the imperishable, and this mortal body must put on immortality. When the perishable puts on the imperishable, and the mortal puts on immortality, then shall come to pass the saying that is written: "Death is swallowed up in victory." (1 Corinthians 15:52–54)

The meaning of death is that the crucified and buried God, Jesus the Christ, who has died and risen from the dead, is the door to life. Jesus said it Himself to Mary as He approached the grave of her brother, Lazarus: "I am the resurrection and the life. Whoever believes in Me, though he die, yet shall he live, and everyone who lives and believes in Me shall never die" (John 11:25–26). Jesus' death is the only meaning that death could ever possess.

QUESTIONS FOR DISCUSSION

How have you personally distanced yourself or been distanced by modern practices from the reality of death? What impact has this had on the experience of death in your life?

There are various ways in which we distance ourselves or are distanced from death. These include never seeing or touching a dead human body; not attending funerals; not caring for the bodies of our deceased loved ones; sending the dying to hospitals or other places where we avoid their dying; never talking about death; and the list goes on. The impact of such distancing from death is that death becomes simply a problem for us to deal with rather than something that God makes a meaningful part of our journey to the true life of God's eternal reign in Christ.

How is death for you simply a problem to be addressed?

Individual answers will vary. Death is a problem when we engage death and dying apart from how God deals with death through the death and resurrection of Jesus by which death becomes a meaningful part of the Creator's story from beginning to end. Death then becomes a part of our participation in God's story.

Have you ever thought about the reality that you are always in communion with death? How does that make you feel?

Reflect on the fact that we are in communion with death constantly: the dead food we eat; the dying air we breathe; the dying and decaying of our bodies; the death of animals, plants, and people all around us (even if we don't see it); the death cries of the planet (volcanoes, earthquakes, floods, typhoons and hurricanes, and so forth).

What is the meaning of death?

The meaning of death is that Jesus is the way, the truth, and the life. No one comes to the Father except through Him. And the only way to get to the Father through Jesus is through Jesus' Passover from death to life. We have to enter into His death and resurrection. When our spiritual and physical death is subsumed (baptized) into His death, then our death simply becomes part of our journey to the Father. Then our death becomes meaningful.

The Cross as the Sign of Victory Over Death

The cross was an incredibly inhumane form of capital punishment, perhaps the most inhumane form imaginable.[86] Jesus died this humiliating and scandalous death. So how could the cross be a symbol of victory over death? Yet, in the preaching of the New Testament Christian community and in the Early Church's life, it became *the* verbal and eventually visible symbol of the victory of Jesus and those incorporated into Him over death.

Notice that it is not the empty tomb that became the symbol of victory. No one I know walks around with an empty tomb hanging around his or her neck. The empty tomb of itself was not good news for those who experienced it. In Mark's Gospel the women flee the tomb with trembling (Mark 16:8), and in John's Gospel, even after Mary Magdalene witnesses to the disciples that she has seen the living Lord, they are still afraid (John 20:19).

Thus, Luther said of the cross and resurrection, "If Christ's life and suffering were not comprehended in the [preached] Word to which faith might cling, they would have availed nothing, for all those who were eyewitnesses received no benefit from their experience, or only very little."[87] Only through

---

86   Consider the gruesome images from the movie *The Passion of the Christ*. See also Gerard Stanley, *He Was Crucified* (St. Louis: Concordia Publishing House, 2009).

87   LW 52:34; cf. 415 BC, 4605, *Sermo catecheticus in pascha*, pp. 59, 721–24.

the proclamation of the Word did they believe that the Jesus who had died and now risen from the dead was the Messiah and the Son of God, Lord of the living and the dead.

The Emmaus disciples only recognized the risen and ruling Lord through the Scriptures and the breaking of the bread (Luke 24:23–35). They recognized Him through the Scriptures by hearing the promises of God in the Old Testament fulfilled specifically in Christ's Passion, His Passover from death to life through His crucifixion, death, burial, and resurrection. They recognized and believed in the Lord through the peaceful and merciful breaking of the bread.

In the Word spoken and the meal encounter, Jesus showed Himself to be the Suffering Servant, the Messiah, the Son of God. They knew that God had exalted Jesus back on high to His authority and rule (Philippians 2:5–11). The cross is the last symbol of this Passover from death to life. Thus, it became the primary sign of this Passover and of Jesus' victory over death. The crucified Jesus and the triumphant Lord are one and the same. The cross is a symbol of both Jesus' suffering and death *and* His victory over sin, evil, and death.

Jesus' victory over sin, evil, and death is something He worked from inside of death. When Jesus succumbed to death on the cross, He descended into death as the Son of God and Lord of Life who burst death open from the inside. Death could not hold the Author of life. The great patristic preacher John Chrysostom put it this way in an Easter homily attributed to him:

> Let no one fear death, for the Death of our Savior has set us free.
> He has destroyed it by enduring it.
> He destroyed Hell when He descended into it.
> He put it into an uproar even as it tasted of His flesh.
> Isaiah foretold this when he said,
> "You, O Hell, have been troubled by encountering Him below."
> Hell was in an uproar because it was done away with.
> It was in an uproar because it is mocked.
> It was in an uproar, for it is destroyed.
> It is in an uproar, for it is annihilated.
> It is in an uproar, for it is now made captive.
> Hell took a body, and discovered God.
> It took earth, and encountered Heaven.

It took what it saw, and was overcome by what it did not see.

O death, where is thy sting?

O Hell, where is thy victory?

Christ is Risen, and you, o death, are annihilated![88]

The cross, that most ancient sign of cruel punishment and death, has become the sign of victory over death because Christ's death destroyed death's power and Christ's resurrection left it annihilated. As the writer to the Hebrews proclaims, "Since therefore the children share in flesh and blood, He Himself likewise partook of the same things, that through death He might destroy the one who has the power of death, that is, the devil, and deliver all those who through fear of death were subject to lifelong slavery" (Hebrews 2:14–15). Christ's cross is a sign of victory for all who are under the power of death because through His death on the cross He is the victor over death.

How then did Jesus undo death from the inside out? Death's power is supplied by sin, hatred, evil, and the devil. Christ entered into death as the opposite: righteousness, love, goodness, life itself, and the living God. By doing so, He undoes death from the inside out. He displayed this love and goodness in the way He entered His suffering and death on the cross: willingly, without regard for Himself or His own life. As Paul says in Galatians 1:4, Christ "gave Himself for our sins to deliver us from the present evil age, according to the will of our God and Father." Jesus willingly gave Himself up to death for the life of the world. Why did God will this for His Son, Jesus Christ? He willed it because He did not create sin, evil, and death. He is the Lord of Life, the one to whom life belongs by His very nature. God did not desire or create death. God created and rejoices in life. He gave Himself up to death in order that He might forever destroy death for us and give us life that lasts forever. Death for those incorporated into Jesus is forever transformed by death's encounter with the One who is life itself.

Through His encounter with death, Jesus shows Himself to be the great Suffering Servant and reveals that servanthood is at the very heart of God's identity. God's identity and power are made perfect in weakness (2 Corinthians 12:9) as the great servant of all. Now, through His suffering and Passion, the body of Jesus shares in this servanthood that is at the center of God's

---

88   John Chrysostom, Easter homily.

identity. The glory that belongs to the Suffering Servant Son of God, united to the human nature of Jesus from the point of His incarnation, now is revealed as belonging to the body of Jesus completely. His body is transformed through His suffering to reveal the identity and glory of God. The One who gave Himself over to death is the One who thereby as God conquers death.

How can we not but proclaim the Lord's death until He comes! Our deaths are now identified with the death of Christ. As Alexander Schmemann says:

> What does it mean to say that we are "dying in Christ"
> (1 Corinthians 15:18) . . . if not that his own unique death,
> the only deathless death, is given to us as our own death—
> that our death is accepted into Christ's death so as to be
> purified, healed, freed of death itself? The death that enters
> into his death is purified, healed, and liberated from death
> as corruption and separation, from the death whose "sting is
> sin" (1 Corinthians 15:56). It becomes the entrance not into
> death, nor even into some mysterious "survival," but into
> unity with Christ, who is the Life of all life.[89]

The servant of all, Christ Jesus, God in the flesh, reveals the life of love that destroys death. To that servant's deathless death God unites our living and our dying. The Suffering Servant's cross permeates the living and dying of all things. It is the hope toward which the whole creation longs. It is the sign of victory for all of God's creation.

QUESTIONS FOR DISCUSSION

How is the cross a symbol of both the power of death and Jesus' victory over death?

Consider who dies on the cross: God's Word made flesh, the Son of God, Jesus. The cross, as a most inhumane form of capital punishment, embodies the sinfulness of humanity as it kills the One sent from the Father, full of grace and truth. We crucified the Lord of glory (1 Corinthians 2:8). Death's power is revealed in that it kills the Author of life, the One through whom all things came into being. It is the

---

89   Schmemann, *The Liturgy of Death*, 90.

primary symbol of the power of death and shows why death must be subdued. Yet, through the cross, the supreme instrument of death, the Son of God subdues the very thing that seeks to destroy Him. And so it becomes the symbol of victory over death. Human sinfulness and evil, witnessed in the crucifixion of the Author of life, cannot overcome Him. Death cannot kill the Author of life. In the resurrection of Jesus, the cross becomes the symbol of Jesus' victory through God's love, forgiveness, mercy, and grace toward His creatures. The symbol of death is simultaneously the symbol of life. Various crosses emphasize one aspect or the other, but they all carry this dual emphasis.

How does Jesus' victory over death lead you to live confidently and hopefully in the world surrounded by death?

Romans 6:8–11 says it all: "Now if we have died with Christ, we believe that we will also live with Him. We know that Christ, being raised from the dead, will never die again; death no longer has dominion over Him. For the death He died He died to sin, once for all, but the life He lives He lives to God. So you also must consider yourselves dead to sin and alive to God in Christ Jesus." Paul tells us to consider ourselves dead to sin and alive to God. Jesus' victory over death leads us to live confidently in this way. In Jesus we are dead to sin and alive to God and our hope is for life after our days here on this earth are ended in the new heavens and the new earth.

What does it mean to you that since the day of your Baptism, you are dying in Christ?

The two options are very stark: dying apart from God, or dying through God's dying and rising. Which would you choose? Death—spiritual, physical, and eternal—apart from God leads to an eternity of dying, shriveling up into a pathetic self-consuming wraith of oneself. Dying in Christ is always dying in His Passover from death to life. It is a dying that leads to new life in God—God creating the new out of the old nothing. To be dying in Christ since the day of your Baptism is simply another way of saying that you have been united to Jesus and His story, and nothing in all creation can separate you from Him and the future that is yours in Him.

The Creator's Final Molding of the Clay— Your Victory Over Death in Your Resurrection

For human beings, death is meaningless. It is the great chasm of separation between the triune God and humans. Only God can transform death into a meaningful reality, something He does through the death and resurrection of His Son, Christ Jesus. In His Son, God has taken up the creative act once again. What we, His human creatures, malformed in our rebellion against God in Adam and Eve, God re-created in His Word made flesh, Jesus.

As we saw in the first chapter, our entire lives are the staging ground for God's great work in our own death when we become clay in the hands of our Creator and are fashioned by Him after the image of the one true living human being: His Son, Jesus Christ. Death and resurrection are the great pottery wheel of God. Through them God re-creates us to be the wondrous, glorified creatures He intended us to be.

The resurrection of your body is a mystery to you. St. Paul indicates as much:

> Behold! I tell you a mystery. We shall not all sleep, but we shall all be changed, in a moment, in the twinkling of an eye, at the last trumpet. For the trumpet will sound, and the dead will be raised imperishable, and we shall be changed. (1 Corinthians 15:51–52)

It is certainly a mystery because we don't know what our resurrected existence will look like, what it will mean for us to be changed. But it is also a mystery because we do know that our resurrected bodies will be conformed to Jesus and His resurrected body. His resurrection is the basis and the pattern for our resurrection. Christ in us, filling us and our lives, is the basis for our resurrection, as Paul says in Colossians 1:25–28 concerning his ministry:

> I became a minister . . . to make the word of God fully known, the mystery hidden for ages and generations but now revealed to His saints. To them God chose to make known how great among the Gentiles are the riches of the glory of this mystery, which is Christ in you, the hope of glory. Him we proclaim, warning everyone and teaching everyone with all wisdom, that we may present everyone mature in Christ.

What it will mean for us to be raised from death is a mystery, beyond our comprehension in this life before death. But we do know that the mystery entails that the life of the one man who has been raised from the dead, Christ Jesus, will fill and enliven our resurrected bodies. This goes far beyond the immortality of our souls. We will live in bodies glorified like Christ's body when God frees His creatures from bondage to physical death. Paul makes this very clear in one of the central passages that speaks to the day of resurrection:

> So is it with the resurrection of the dead. What is sown is perishable; what is raised is imperishable. It is sown in dishonor; it is raised in glory. It is sown in weakness; it is raised in power. It is sown a natural body; it is raised a spiritual body. If there is a natural body, there is also a spiritual body. Thus it is written, "The first man Adam became a living being"; the last Adam became a life-giving spirit. But it is not the spiritual that is first but the natural, and then the spiritual. The first man was from the earth, a man of dust; the second man is from heaven. As was the man of dust, so also are those who are of the dust, and as is the man of heaven, so also are those who are of heaven. Just as we have borne the image of the man of dust, we shall also bear the image of the man of heaven. (1 Corinthians 15:42–49)

We will bear the image of the man of heaven: Jesus Christ. This is the mystery: that our resurrected bodily lives will bear the image in some way of the glorified God in the flesh, Jesus.

Every Sunday when you say, in the words of the Nicene Creed, "I look for the resurrection of the dead," or, in the words of the Apostles' Creed, "I believe in the resurrection of the body," you confess that God will raise your body in the image of His Son, Jesus. This has been your hope since the day of your Baptism, when the Church applied Paul's words in Romans 6:3–5 to you:

> Do you not know that all of us who have been baptized into Christ Jesus were baptized into His death? We were buried therefore with Him by baptism into death, in order that, just as Christ was raised from the dead by the glory of the Father, we too might walk in newness of life. *For if we have been united with Him in a death like*

His, we shall certainly be united with Him in a resurrection like His. (emphasis added)

Since your Baptism day, the heavenly Father has been immersing you into death, the death of His Son. Through Baptism we participate in the death of death as the end, as hopeless meaninglessness, as the great enemy. Through Baptism into Christ, the Father transforms human life and death into the central, loving shape of human life.

This pattern of dying and rising is, in the human Christ Jesus, the pattern of human life. His dying and rising is the substance of human life and the meaning of our life and death. This is why Paul can confess to the Philippians, "For to me to live is Christ, and to die is gain" (Philippians 1:21), and to the Romans, "For if we live, we live to the Lord, and if we die, we die to the Lord. So then, whether we live or whether we die, we are the Lord's. For to this end Christ died and lived again, that He might be Lord both of the dead and of the living" (Romans 14:8–9). Through your Baptism your life is now lived in Christ alone. Your dying is now united to Christ's death and resurrection. As a baptized child of God, whether you live or you die, Jesus is your Lord in both life and death.

Our funerals simply recognize that the journey of death and resurrection in Christ begun in Baptism has reached its completion in this life, the penultimate stage before the final completion at Jesus' resurrection. It is our life in Christ, the life of God in Christ given to us in our Baptism, that we celebrate at funerals. In our funerals we tell the story of our bodily and spiritual journeys from Baptism to grave to resurrection from the grave, of our journey through life to death and back to life in Christ. It is the journey we have been making our entire lives, in the company of the entire Church, of all the baptized. And now the baptized accompany us as we reach the final threshold of our journey, our earthly death, and wait for the end of the journey at the resurrection of our bodies. As the Church celebrates the funerals of the ones the Father loves, all of us enter "together with the deceased brother or sister into the deathless death of Christ."[90]

The interim state between the death of our bodies and the resurrection of all flesh is not when we will reach the fulfillment of our Baptism in the death-

---

90   Ibid., 85.

less death of Christ, His eternal resurrection. The journey's end is not this interim state. This is simply a time of waiting for the resurrection, both for our spirits and our bodies. Because we are still waiting in the interim state, it is not the end or goal. The goal of the journey is the resurrection of our bodies and the union of body and soul in the life of the risen Christ.

When the question "Where are they now?" arises as we approach our own death or experience the death of someone we love, we shouldn't focus on their grave or on the place of rest in which their spirit may be. Instead, we focus our eyes where the Lord of death and life is. For where He is, there are all those baptized into His death and resurrection. Until the resurrection, their life is now hidden in Christ with God. You'll find your loved ones where Jesus is, hidden in Him. As Paul says in 1 Corinthians 10:16–17, "The cup of blessing that we bless, is it not a participation in the blood of Christ? The bread that we break, is it not a participation in the body of Christ? Because there is one bread, we who are many are one body, for we all partake of the one bread." Wherever Christ has promised to be, when you want to know where your deceased baptized loved ones are, look there.

QUESTIONS FOR DISCUSSION

How would you describe what it will look like for you to bear the image of the risen Jesus in your resurrected body?

It doesn't mean that you will look exactly like Jesus, the mirror image. Then you wouldn't be you. In many ways we are speculating here, but think of the things that are characteristic of Jesus as the Son of God and the one faithful human; you will show those characteristics in your person. Jesus is pure joy. You will show pure joy. Jesus is completely truthful. You will always behave and speak truthfully. Jesus is the love of God. You will radiate the love of God. Jesus is the light of creation. You will reflect the light of Jesus in your body. Those are just some examples of how you will bear the image of the risen Jesus.

How does knowing Jesus as the Lord of death and life enable you to enter into daily dying and rising?

Jesus is victor over death's power and sting in all its forms. Our daily dying and rising are part of the reality of His death and resurrection and so are surrounded by His victory. Dying to our own sinful desires, sacrificing our own interests and wishes so as to serve our neighbor in love, and suffering the effects of sin and evil through the crosses and persecution others inflict upon us is possible because Christ reigns over sin, evil, death, and hell. We can walk the way of daily repentance because Jesus is a forerunner, paving the way past sin, temptation, and death (see Hebrews 12).

If your funeral is simply the final earthly stage in your journey, then how ought you to plan your funeral?

You should plan your funeral as a journey that you and your body are making toward the final kingdom of God. This journey is only possible in Christ. You are laying your body at rest until Christ calls it to new life when He returns. Your soul and spirit will rest in the presence of God until that final day. As you prepare to make this journey, you should be surrounded by the Body of Christ who is making the same journey with you. The Church should participate in and celebrate this journey in Christ with you. Read the Word that rehearses the new life in Christ and the kingdom to come. Sing hymns that tell the story of your baptismal life in Christ. Ritualize the funeral with words and actions that evoke your journey. This would include your body's journey from its initial place of rest (ideally, your home) to the church to the final place of rest such as a cemetery. All of these are ways you can prepare for the final journey in your funeral.

Why should we look to the Lord's Supper—not "up to heaven"—to see our deceased loved ones who are baptized into and believers in the triune God?

While our baptized and believing deceased members of Christ's Body are at rest in the presence of Jesus, we will finally see them again in Christ at the end of the pilgrimage: the new heavens and new earth that God is preparing. The Lord's Supper is the foretaste of that great feast of God in the rule and reign He will establish. By faith through the Word, we are united with all the saints when we assemble at His invitation at the Supper that He has established as the foretaste of the feast to come. In anticipation of that great feast where we will see them again, we "see" them again when we gather to celebrate the Lord's Supper as they join us in the great "holy, holy, holy" around the throne of the Lamb. So, I look forward each week to "meeting" again with my sainted (baptized and believing) grandparents, father, father-in-law, and the countless saints of the ages, known and unknown to me, who join me around the table of the Lord.

The Resurrection of the Cosmos

Looking for our sainted dead and finding them wherever Christ is starts to expand our vision of the resurrection. Often our vision is much too small, turned in only on ourselves, our death, and the hope of our resurrection. But the resurrection of the Word of life encompasses every aspect of the creation that the Father brought into being through Him. It is an eschatological vision that includes God's lordship over all creation. Paul sings such an ode to the cosmological significance of Jesus' resurrection in 1 Corinthians 15:20–28:

> But in fact Christ has been raised from the dead, the firstfruits of those who have fallen asleep. For as by a man came death, by a man has come also the resurrection of the dead. For as in Adam all die, so also in Christ shall all be made alive. But each in his own order: Christ the firstfruits, then at His coming those who belong to Christ. Then comes the end, when He delivers the kingdom to God the Father after destroying every rule and every authority and power. For He must reign until He has put all His enemies under His feet. The last enemy to be destroyed is death. For "God has put all things in subjection under His feet." But when it says, "all things are put in subjection," it is plain that He is excepted who put all things in subjection under Him. When all things are subjected to Him, then the Son Himself will also be subjected to Him who put all things in subjection under Him, that God may be all in all.

Jesus' resurrection doesn't concern just our resurrection, but the restoration of life from God for the entire universe. It is a cosmic event: everything in subjection to the Prince of life, that God may be all in all. Imagine resurrection through a panoramic camera lens. God calls us to see the resurrection with such a panoramic vision. Jesus' resurrection brings with it this "resurrection" or restoration of all creation (Acts 3:19–21). Paul describes this cosmic restoration as the uniting of "all things in Him, things in heaven and things on earth" (Ephesians 1:9–10); "through Him to reconcile to Himself all things, whether on earth or in heaven, making peace by the blood of His cross" (Colossians 1:20); and finally, in Romans 8:19–23:

> For the creation waits with eager longing for the revealing of the sons of God. For the creation was subjected to futility, not willingly, but because of Him who subjected it, in hope that the creation itself will be set free from its bondage to corruption and obtain the freedom of the glory of the children of God. For we know that the whole creation has been groaning together in the pains of childbirth until now. And not only the creation, but we ourselves, who have the firstfruits of the Spirit, groan inwardly as we wait eagerly for adoption as sons, the redemption of our bodies.

The redemption of the body, our resurrection, is part of the greater freeing of the cosmos from bondage through the enthronement of the resurrected Lord. We groan with the cosmos for the day of resurrection. In Peter's words, "According to His promise we are waiting for new heavens and a new earth in which righteousness dwells" (2 Peter 3:13).

In hope for this great restoration, the Church continually should cry, "Maranatha—come, Lord Jesus!" (see 1 Corinthians 16:22). Every time the Church cries, "Come, Lord," it is crying for Him to come and establish His rule and reign, to usher in the resurrection of the dead, and to restore all things. It is our cry for the entire creation, our longing for the entire creation to experience the new life of the resurrected Christ.

We make the same cry every time we speak the Second Petition of the prayer our Lord gave us: "Thy kingdom come." We are praying for His kingdom to come among us now, as Luther notes in his Small Catechism, but we are also praying for His kingdom to come at the end of time. We are praying for the consummation of all things in Christ, for the uniting of all things in the new heavens and the new earth in the life of the Lamb who was slain but now lives.

Every aspect of our lives now should be the plea of this prayer: "Come, Lord; Your rule and reign come." In this phrase is embedded the meaning of life and death: that everything in this life will be put to death and brought to new life in Christ. Our living, the meaning of our lives, and the life of everything in the entire universe is reconciled to God in Christ and brought to its final fulfillment in Him. This is the cosmic vision of the resurrection!

Feasting is how the Scriptures portray the celebration of the resurrected life. Isaiah prophesies such a feast on the mountain of the Lord, a symbol of the establishment of God's reign:

> On this mountain the LORD of hosts will make for all peoples a
> feast of rich food, a feast of well-aged wine, of rich food full of
> marrow, of aged wine well refined. And He will swallow up on this
> mountain the covering that is cast over all peoples, the veil that is
> spread over all nations. He will swallow up death forever; and the
> Lord GOD will wipe away tears from all faces, and the reproach of
> His people He will take away from all the earth, for the LORD has
> spoken. (Isaiah 25:6–8)

Eating at the feast of rich food and well-aged wine is the sign of participation in the resurrection kingdom of God where death is swallowed up forever. You'll know you are in the resurrection kingdom if you are eating the food that never dies, that comes from the source of life itself. Jesus Himself describes the kingdom of God with the parable of the wedding feast to which all are invited (Matthew 22:1–14). So the Church's meals on earth become signs of the coming rule and reign of God and of the resurrected life. Every week that congregations celebrate the Sacrament, the Church remembers this cosmic vision of the resurrection and participates in its foretaste as the baptized eat together.

That eating together includes the meal that the Lord instituted, the Lord's Supper, as the remembrance of the coming of His kingdom: "Do this in remembrance of Me." When we remember a person who is no longer present—or an event we once shared together—that person and moment almost feels real for an instant. But Christ's resurrection means that whenever we remember His death for us in Holy Communion, He is truly present with and within us—not just for the instant we eat and drink, but always. And God gifts the Church with such divine remembering in the Lord's Supper, the remembrance of Christ Jesus.

When we eat Jesus' body and blood, God remembers us in the life of His beloved Son. Through our participation in the Lord's Supper liturgy and in the meal, we keep in remembrance all those who participate in the Supper of the Lord. All those who are in Christ, whether living or dead, are kept in remembrance, united with us in this living meal. That is because it is a meal of the crucified and risen Lord. It is a meal of the resurrection. And all those who eat the meal of the resurrected Lord are united through the bread and wine to the Risen One. Through the resurrection Supper of the Lord we are in communion with all those who will rise with Christ on the day of His appearing and join in the marriage feast of the Lamb in His kingdom that will have no end.

When we enter into the feasting room of God's kingdom, surrounded by the entire renewed cosmos, our journey into the death of Christ will have reached its fulfillment. Then our death truly will have been swallowed up by Life. Throughout this life we walk the path of death toward life, learning to die and to rise. The theologian John Behr writes:

> The life of the baptized is one of learning to die, learning, that is, specifically to take up the Cross of Christ. Death will finally reveal in which direction my heart is ordered. When I am returned to the dust, then, and only then, do I finally experience my complete and utter frailty and weakness. Then, and only then, do I become clay, clay fashioned by the Hands of God into living flesh. And so, it is only then that the God whose strength is made perfect in weakness can finally be the Creator: taking dust from the earth which I now am and mixing in his power, he now finally fashions a true, living, human being. When this happens the act begun in Baptism is completed.[91]

Amen! Maranatha! Come, Lord Jesus.

QUESTIONS FOR DISCUSSION

How do you see the creation groaning for renewal and a new creation?
I grew up in Cincinnati, Ohio. I remember being entranced as a young child by a memorial at my hometown zoo to the very last passenger pigeon that ever lived on the earth. She was named Martha and she died in the Cincinnati Zoo in 1914. Millions of passenger pigeons once flew

---

91   Behr, *Becoming Human*, 66–69.

in massive flocks above the earth. But human sin and evil led to their demise and extinction. The passenger pigeon's extinction is just one example of the creation's groaning for renewal and new creation. I hope that the Lord will see fit to resurrect the passenger pigeon in the new earth and that in my glorified state I'll get to see the glorified species–sibling of Martha.

What does it mean to make every aspect of our lives a cry for the Lord to come?

First, it means that this cry should be upon our lips as often as possible. We should consciously call for the Lord to come and so train ourselves to live in perpetual hope of His coming. Second, it means that everything we do is done in the recognition that Christ will come again, soon. We should be prepared, repenting of our sinful state in anticipation of His judgment, and longing with joy to see His reappearing, because we know He will lead us into His eternal kingdom (Matthew 25:1–13).

How is the Lord's Supper a meal that celebrates the cosmic renewal that will come with Jesus' return?

We know that the promise of the Creator's Word, Jesus' return, brings with it the renewal of all creation (Romans 8:19–23). The bread and wine that our Lord uses in His Supper as the signs of the Kingdom that He will establish are both a staple food (bread) and a sign of celebration and joy (wine). These very basic foods symbolize the creation God made and point us toward the renewal of creation itself in the new earth of God's kingdom. In a sense, in the bread and wine we see a microcosm of the whole earth and the entire cosmos, renewed by the power of the Word.

How is the Lord's Supper already a participation in the resurrection community of God?

In Luke's Gospel, the Lord tells us that He will not eat the fruit of the vine again until the kingdom of God comes (Luke 22:18). It will not come finally until Christ returns. The Lord's Supper is the foretaste of that eternal banquet, and all who have partaken throughout time of the one bread and the one cup (1 Corinthians 10:14–19) are united as one

Body of Christ. We already participate in the resurrection body of Christ and so "meet" all the saints at the Lord's Supper.

How is the cry "Come, Lord Jesus" a cry for a meaningful death (a death in Christ's deathless death), a cry for God to finish His pottery work (you) on the Last Day?

The cry "Come, Lord Jesus" is a cry for the Father to finish His story in Christ, to bring it to completion. We participate in that story, and so when we cry this we are crying for our story to be brought to completion in Christ. The completion of that story includes death in Christ. We cry for the only meaningful death possible, one that leads to the eternal kingdom of the living God, or the deathless death of Christ for us. We cry to the Father to bring His pottery molding to completion: form us to be living clay in Christ Jesus our Lord.

Resurrection Hope in Uncertain Situations

Earlier in this chapter I noted that from the moment of our Baptism, we have lived in the hope that God will raise our bodies in Jesus' resurrection. Our Baptism pushes us into living the trajectory of Jesus' baptismal, resurrection story. But many things in life challenge our confidence that the story's trajectory will be followed to the end. Among those challenges are the loss of a child's life through miscarriage or stillbirth. These profound losses create uncertainty and doubt.

After a mother has carried her own living child in her womb for some period of time, the death of the child through miscarriage or stillbirth causes her—and the father—significant sorrow, pain, suffering, and loss. These experiences of suffering raise existential questions for grieving parents: Why did the Lord of Life allow this to happen? Since my child was not born, he or she was not baptized. Did my child believe? Was he or she saved? Does the promise of the resurrection apply to my child?

There is no way to avoid the struggle for faith and trust that confronts parents who lose a child in miscarriage or stillbirth. The death of their child before birth prevented their child's entrance into the story of resurrection through

Baptism (Mark 16:16). So they are brought into conflict with the God who says, "I am the way, and the truth, and the life" (John 14:6).

There is no way to resolve the conflict and eradicate all uncertainty and doubt about the promise of the resurrection. But as parents wrestle through the conflict, confronted by sorrow, anger, and despair, the promises of the God who raised His Son, Jesus, from the dead can be spoken to them about their children.

While the promise of Baptism can't be spoken, the story of the resurrecting God can. When Peter first preaches the Gospel following the Pentecost fire in Acts, he says, "Repent and be baptized every one of you in the name of Jesus Christ for the forgiveness of your sins, and you will receive the gift of the Holy Spirit. For the promise is for you and for your children and for all who are far off, everyone whom the Lord our God calls to Himself" (Acts 2:38–39).

The promise of new life, while received through Baptism, is for all the children of the families to whom the promise of Christ is proclaimed. There is no qualifier or exception. The promise is proclaimed to children both before they are born and after they are born. In fact, Jesus Himself says that one's primary identity as a member of the kingdom of God is that of a child.

> And they were bringing children to Him that He might touch
> them, and the disciples rebuked them. But when Jesus saw it, He
> was indignant and said to them, "Let the children come to Me;
> do not hinder them, for to such belongs the kingdom of God.
> Truly, I say to you, whoever does not receive the kingdom of God
> like a child shall not enter it." And He took them in His arms and
> blessed them, laying His hands on them. (Mark 10:13–16)

The Lord will raise children, children who died at many different ages and at many stages of development, as those who inherit His kingdom. Parents grieving the death of their child in utero can cling to these promises of the risen Lord in their struggle for faith regarding the resurrection hope for their unbaptized children. They can cling to the Lord who says He is the way, the truth, and the life for all who come to the Father.[92]

---

92   For a full discussion of resurrection hope when a child is lost through miscarriage or stillbirth, see Kathryn Ziegler Weber, *Never Forsaken: God's Mercy in the Midst of Miscarriage* (St. Louis: Concordia Publishing House, 2018).

QUESTION FOR DISCUSSION

What should you say to those who have suffered a miscarriage or stillbirth?

First, you should say nothing. You should simply let them mourn and, often, lament to God. They need a shoulder to cry on, a body to lean on, a friend in Christ to hear all their emotions: sorrow, anger, frustration, and grief. Then, you can say, "Jesus is the way and the truth and the life. No one comes to the Father except through Him" (see John 14:6). All that you say should point to the crucified and risen Jesus as the hope for those who have experienced the tragedy of a miscarriage or stillbirth.

The Judgment

The resurrection of all human beings, dead and those still living at Christ's appearing, ushers in the final judgment—including that of the evil angels (2 Peter 2:4). Jesus describes the scene in Matthew's Gospel:

> When the Son of Man comes in His glory, and all the angels with Him, then He will sit on His glorious throne. Before Him will be gathered all the nations, and He will separate people one from another as a shepherd separates the sheep from the goats. And He will place the sheep on His right, but the goats on the left. Then the King will say to those on His right, "Come, you who are blessed by My Father, inherit the kingdom prepared for you from the foundation of the world." . . . Then He will say to those on His left, "Depart from Me, you cursed, into the eternal fire prepared for the devil and his angels." . . . And these will go away into eternal punishment, but the righteous into eternal life. (Matthew 25:31–34, 41, 46)

The resurrected life is fully realized when those who believe in the Father, Jesus Christ as the life of the world, and the Holy Spirit enter into the new heavens and the new earth with Christ as Lord and Ruler. Those who fail to believe in the triune God and reject His gracious Word are separated from God and God's kingdom and reside in that place of separation, hell. For those who believe in Jesus' name there is no fear that at the judgment they will not enter the new heaven and earth that He has prepared for them.

The final judgment elicits a difficult realization: some will be eternally separated from God and God's kingdom. Many Christians find this a difficult reality to reconcile with the God of grace made known in Jesus. There is nothing wrong with desiring that everyone enter into the rule and reign of God. And most of us personally know someone who is not a believer whom we would desire for God to bring into His kingdom.

So, will every human being who has ever lived be saved? The biblical answer is no. There are at least two reasons for this. As we have noted, God accomplishes the establishment of His reign in His Son through the judgment. Jesus serves as the agent of judgment Himself. Images of the judgment as the final entry point into the new heavens and the new earth or into hell are prevalent (see Matthew 8; 13; Mark 9). Judgment will occur.

Second, entrance into the kingdom of the resurrected life means that our old human will and our old lives must be submitted to God's will and God's life. Such submission of our old human will only happens through God's killing of that will. Our old human will has to die before we can live according to God's will and by His life-giving Word. Repentance is this killing of our old will and raising of a new person that the Spirit accomplishes in us through the Word.

In repentance, first the Holy Spirit works to turn us from our old evil ways and to reject our lives of evil unbelief. Second, the Spirit turns us to God in trust and, from that trust in God, leads us to submit to His Word and will and to live out the fruit of the Spirit, a new way of life. Our final repentance will take place when we enter into the kingdom of God and are radically transformed by the resurrecting and life-giving Word. The way we formerly lived in the old earth will be radically different from the way that we will live in Christ in the new heavens and the new earth.

Through grace and love in Christ Jesus, God seeks to transform human creatures. When the Holy Spirit creates trust in His grace and love in Christ, a new way of life flows from that trusting relationship like fruit growing on a healthy tree. But some people simply refuse God's loving activity through His Word and continue in their rebellion against God. They willfully resist. The grace and love of God through His Word does not transform them. We can certainly desire and pray for such a transformation to take place for all human beings, but there are some who will not be transformed and will not be saved.[93]

If universalism (the notion that everyone will enter the eternal rule and reign of God) is impossible, then that means some people face eternal separation from God—the judgment of damnation. Paul describes it in 2 Thessalonians 1:8–10 when he says that "those who do not know God and . . . those who do not obey the gospel of our Lord Jesus . . . will suffer the punishment of eternal destruction, away from the presence of the Lord and from the glory of His might, when He comes on that day."

Damnation is simply separation from the loving presence of the God who is life. God excludes those who will not trust in the loving life of God in Christ Jesus from communion with Him. They are left to their ongoing unbelief and increasingly turn in on themselves, finding their life only in themselves, burning with their own preoccupation and narcissism, isolated from the life of God.

If you are familiar with the figure of Gollum in the Lord of the Rings trilogy, he approximates well the depiction of the damned: one who increasingly, narcissistically feeds only on his own desires and wants and shrivels into a pathetic mockery of his former self. So lies the fate of those eternally separated from God.

QUESTION FOR DISCUSSION

How should we talk about and use the biblical teaching on the judgment of God in our speech to one another and to unbelievers?

We should never use it to scare someone into believing in the living God. It won't work. Only the Good News of the Gospel can elicit and bring faith to life. The judgment of God should be used as a contrast to the good news of God's establishment of His kingdom, where all who live in Him through Christ will dwell eternally. The judgment of God contrasts with this eternal kingdom of God and should lead people to see sharply the hope of the future that the risen Lord promises to all who trust in Him.

---

93   I am indebted to J. Richard Middleton's thoughts on universal salvation in *A New Heaven and a New Earth: Reclaiming Biblical Eschatology*, 207–9.

The Place of Eternal Separation: Hell

Their fate is for God to exile them to the place of eternal separation from Him: hell. Hell is the opposite of that place where the resurrected will live with God, having brought heaven down to the new earth. Hell is separation from God and from living with others and with the whole renewed creation.

The Scriptures describe hell in other ways: everlasting fire (Matthew 18:8); everlasting punishment (Matthew 25:46); tribulation and anguish (Romans 2:9); torments (Luke 16:23); the fire that shall not be quenched (Mark 9:43–44); weeping and gnashing of teeth (Matthew 8:12). All the suffering, pain, and narcissism of this life will be amplified in hell because the presence of God's light will not shine there to drive away all forms of human evil and misery.

There will be fire. But will it be actual flames or are the Scriptures speaking metaphorically? The description of hell as a place of fire can be interpreted in either direction. Given that I find it compelling to see hell as the place of utter isolation and loneliness in separation from God and God's kingdom, I tend to interpret the fires of hell as forms of extreme personal agony and anguish brought on the person by rejecting God and relying solely on him- or herself, rather than actual flames. But we can have different theological opinions about this.

Cut off from communion with God and others, those who are in hell are captive to the dungeons of their own minds. C. S. Lewis's depiction of the emperor Napoleon as residing in hell captures this narcissistic captivity:

> "Two chaps made the journey to see him. They'd started long
> before I came, of course, but I was there when they came back.
> About fifteen thousand years of our time it took them. We've
> picked out the house by now. Just a little pin prick of light and
> nothing else near it for millions of miles."
>
> "But they got there?"
>
> "That's right. He'd built himself a huge house all in the Empire
> style—rows of windows flaming with light, though it only shows
> as a pin prick from where I live."

"Did they see Napoleon?"

"That's right. They went up and looked through one of the windows. Napoleon was there all right."

"What was he doing?"

"Walking up and down—up and down all the time—left-right, left-right—never stopping for a moment. The two chaps watched him for about a year and he never rested. And muttering to himself all the time. 'It was Soult's fault. It was Ney's fault. It was Josephine's fault. It was the fault of the Russians. It was the fault of the English.' Like that all the time. Never stopped for a moment. A little, fat man and he looked kind of tired. But he didn't seem able to stop it."[94]

Turned in on themselves, those in hell, according to Lewis's visualization, become increasingly less physically human and more like waifs and ghosts.[95]

Failing to possess the very physical realities of God's new heavens and new earth, those sent to hell insist on keeping something from the old earth, even if that means misery for them.[96] They can't let go of the old. It is a form of unbelief, a failure to trust in the God of all creation who will grant new life and all things new in the new heavens and the new earth. It is idolatry to hold onto the old earth and the things of it at all cost. For example, holding on to one's usefulness would be a form of this unbelief. In this case a person would only want to live in an afterlife where he or she is useful in some way. In response to this, Lewis writes:

> "No," said the other [the dweller in heaven]. "I can promise you none of these things. No sphere of usefulness: you are not needed there [in heaven] at all. No scope for your talents: only forgiveness for having perverted them. No atmosphere of inquiry, for I will

---

94   C. S. Lewis, *The Great Divorce*, 22.

95   Ibid., 76.

96   Ibid., 69.

bring you to the land not of questions but of answers, and you shall see the face of God."[97]

Lewis's fictional description of heaven and hell reflects Jesus' description in the parable of the rich fool (Luke 12:16–21):

> The land of a rich man produced plentifully, and he thought to himself, "What shall I do, for I have nowhere to store my crops?" And he said, "I will do this: I will tear down my barns and build larger ones, and there I will store all my grain and my goods. And I will say to my soul, 'Soul, you have ample goods laid up for many years; relax, eat, drink, be merry.'" But God said to him, "Fool! This night your soul is required of you, and the things you have prepared, whose will they be?" So is the one who lays up treasure for himself and is not rich toward God.

We cannot hold onto the things of this old creation, whether wealth, possessions, reputation, work, or anything else, in hope that they will carry over into the new heaven and the new earth. God will transform everything from the old creation, putting it to death and making all things new, in the new heaven and earth.

So where is hell? Jesus tells us in His parable about the rich man and Lazarus (Luke 16:19–31) that a great chasm separates hell from the place where God fulfills His promises to Abraham. The rich man lived a life of ease and abundance. Lazarus was a destitute, chronically ill homeless man. They both died. The rich man went to Hades, and Lazarus was carried by angels to Abraham's side. When the formerly rich man seeks comfort in the midst of the agony of Hades, Abraham tells him that the great chasm prevents him from bringing any comfort to the rich man. And of course his earthly riches, which he left behind, are of no assistance to him now. Hell and the new heavens and the new earth are completely divided from each other. God's life fills the new heavens and the new earth. Hell is devoid completely of the life of the Trinity and the peace that comes with living in God's kingdom.

Hell is where God is not; it is not in the new heavens and the new earth! But we shouldn't speculate about its location. Rather, we should make sure that

---

97   Ibid., 43.

we and all our loved ones and neighbors long to see the face of God in Christ eternally. Then, seeking to keep them out of hell, we should proclaim to them the resurrection promise to which the risen Christ bears witness and which He will bring to fulfillment in the eternal kingdom of His Father. It is the new creation of justice, peace, hope, joy, and love. Hell is the exact opposite. To this most beautiful new creation, Christ beckons all.

QUESTION FOR DISCUSSION

If we say hell is the place devoid of the triune God's life-giving presence, what do you understand that to mean?

Many different kinds of answers are possible here. All of those answers should indicate that hell is a place in which there dwells no true life because Jesus, the way, the truth, and the life of God, is not there, and neither are His Father and the Spirit of God. The breath that brings life does not blow in hell.

Our Victorious Hope

Because God raised Jesus from the dead, we live as people of undeniable hope. As Paul prays for the Church in Ephesus:

> [May] the God of our Lord Jesus Christ, the Father of glory,
> . . . give you the Spirit of wisdom and of revelation in the
> knowledge of Him, having the eyes of your hearts enlight-
> ened, that you may know what is the hope to which He has
> called you, what are the riches of His glorious inheritance
> in the saints, and what is the immeasurable greatness of His
> power toward us who believe, according to the working of
> His great might. (Ephesians 1:17–19)

The hope to which He has called you is the glorious inheritance of the saints, the eternal resurrected life in God's rule and reign in Christ. Held firm by that hope, you can learn the art of dying well.

Peter Phan highlights the characteristics of dying well within the embrace of a living hope.[98] First, it means that throughout our life, we can face our own death and the deaths of others squarely in the eye. It will happen and we need not fear. We can own our mortality because Jesus has died our death and our lives are now hidden in His deathless life.

Second, we can live a life fully trusting in God and loving our neighbor because God has freed us from death paralysis. We should not embrace death and make it our friend, but we know that Christ's death has put death into its place and robbed it of its meaninglessness. We can make the most of our living because our death is not the end of all things.

Lastly, we can practice virtues that lead us to a peaceful and holy death. Paul provides us a good list of such virtues: "Put on then, as God's chosen ones, holy and beloved, compassionate hearts, kindness, humility, meekness, and patience" (Colossians 3:12). One might add to the list thankfulness, courage, obedience, trust, and love. In so doing one is preparing not only for a holy death, but for living a good life that leads to a holy death. Trusting the hope of the risen Christ, we can learn the art of dying well.

We live and die in hope, a hope alive in the Lord Jesus. So, Peter begins his first letter:

> Blessed be the God and Father of our Lord Jesus Christ!
> According to His great mercy, He has caused us to be born
> again to a living hope through the resurrection of Jesus
> Christ from the dead, to an inheritance that is imperishable,
> undefiled, and unfading, kept in heaven for you, who by
> God's power are being guarded through faith for a salvation
> ready to be revealed in the last time. In this you rejoice,
> though now for a little while, if necessary, you have been
> grieved by various trials, so that the tested genuineness of
> your faith—more precious than gold that perishes though it
> is tested by fire—may be found to result in praise and glory
> and honor at the revelation of Jesus Christ. (1 Peter 1:3–7)

We have a living hope for the new heavens and the new earth through the resurrection of Jesus.

---

98   Peter Phan, *Living into Death, Dying into Life: A Christian Theology of Death and Life Eternal* (Hobe Sound, FL: Lectio Publishing, 2014), 22–25.

Many things in life can cloud and assail the vibrancy of our resurrection hope. Two that often eviscerate our hope are illness, especially chronic and debilitating illness, and old age. Illnesses like cancer, ALS, Parkinson's disease, and Alzheimer's disease and other forms of dementia can rob those afflicted and those that care for them of hope in this life. Over against the despair and hopelessness that may surface for those struggling against these diseases, we, the Body of Christ, proclaim and witness the hope of the One victorious over all destructive and debilitating sicknesses and illnesses. Anointed with the oil of the Holy Spirit, those battling debilitating illness find their hope in the Jesus anointed with the same life-giving Spirit.[99]

Medical and technological advances have propelled the average life span forward. We live much longer than our forebears, with people regularly reaching the age of 100 and beyond. Yet, the length of time spent in old age is a two-edged sword. After the age of 80 we face increased risk of debilitating illness, chronic pain, loss of sight and hearing, senility and dementia, decreased mobility, and the loss of spouses, family, and friends through death long before we die. The result is that the aged face isolation, despair, loneliness, helplessness, and the loss of any purpose for living. We must acknowledge these debilitations for what they are. They are evil and cause suffering. In the face of such suffering it is appropriate for the sick and aged to cry out as the psalmist did:

> O LORD, God of my salvation, I cry out day and night before You.
> Let my prayer come before You; incline Your ear to my cry! For
> my soul is full of troubles, and my life draws near to Sheol. I am
> counted among those who go down to the pit; I am a man who has
> no strength, like one set loose among the dead, like the slain that
> lie in the grave, like those whom You remember no more, for they
> are cut off from Your hand. (Psalm 88:1–5)

But as we have seen, God does remember us in His Son, Jesus Christ. The woman who was afflicted by a debilitating disease with a flow of blood dared to touch Jesus' garment in the hope of healing. What ensued between them is the source of hope for the sick and aging facing hopelessness: "But the

---

99   Actual anointing of the sick ought to be considered as an option to point the sick to hope in the Lord.

woman, knowing what had happened to her, came in fear and trembling and fell down before Him and told Him the whole truth. And He said to her, 'Daughter, your faith has made you well; go in peace, and be healed of your disease'"(Mark 5:33–34). In the new earth that God the Father will establish under His Son is a tree whose leaves are for the healing of the nations (Revelation 22:2). Our hope is in the Lord who will plant the tree of healing in His kingdom.

Our hope is in the living Lord who will return to establish the resurrection kingdom. First, the risen Christ descends to earth, and then all of the sainted dead will rise. As Paul says, "Each in his own order: Christ the firstfruits, then at His coming those who belong to Christ. Then comes the end, when He delivers the kingdom to God the Father after destroying every rule and every authority and power" (1 Corinthians 15:23–24). The risen Jesus, very much in the flesh, love visible through the nail and spear marks He bears, is our victorious hope.

> Behold! I tell you a mystery. We shall not all sleep, but we shall all be changed, in a moment, in the twinkling of an eye, at the last trumpet. For the trumpet will sound, and the dead will be raised imperishable, and we shall be changed. For this perishable body must put on the imperishable, and this mortal body must put on immortality. When the perishable puts on the imperishable, and the mortal puts on immortality, then shall come to pass the saying that is written: "Death is swallowed up in victory." "O death, where is your victory? O death, where is your sting?" The sting of death is sin, and the power of sin is the law. But thanks be to God, who gives us the victory through our Lord Jesus Christ. (1 Corinthians 15:51–57)

All the baptized believers are more than conquerors!

QUESTION FOR DISCUSSION

Express in your own words Paul's description of the transformation of our bodies and spirits on the Last Day, the putting on of the imperishable and the immortal.

Since we have no complete depiction of what our transformed

bodies and spirits will look like, many answers are possible here. All the answers should point to Christ Jesus as the pattern, form, and image of our transformed persons. We will be incorporated into His resurrected life and so He will share the characteristics of His glorified humanity with us.

The Day Is Surely Drawing Near

1. The day is surely drawing near
   When Jesus, God's anointed,
   In all His power shall appear
   As judge whom God appointed
   Then fright shall banish idle mirth,
   And flames on flames shall ravage earth
   As Scripture long has warned us.

2. The final trumpet then shall sound
   And all the earth be shaken,
   And all who rest beneath the ground
   Shall from their sleep awaken.
   But all who live will in that hour,
   By God's almighty, boundless pow'r,
   Be changed at His commanding.

3. The books are opened then to all,
   A record truly telling
   What each has done, both great and small,
   When he on earth was dwelling,
   And ev'ry heart be clearly seen,
   And all be known as they have been
   In thoughts and words and actions.

4. Then woe to those who scorned the Lord
   And sought but carnal pleasures,
   Who here despised His precious Word
   And loved their earthly treasures!
   With shame and trembling they will stand
   And at the judge's stern command
   To Satan be delivered.

5. My Savior paid the debt I owe
   And for my sin was smitten;
   Within the Book of Life I know
   My name has now been written.
   I will not doubt, for I am free,
   And Satan cannot threaten me;
   There is no condemnation!

6. May Christ our intercessor be
   And through His blood and merit
   Read from His book that we are free
   With all who life inherit.
   Then we shall see Him face to face,
   With all His saints in that blest place
   Which He has purchased for us.

7. O Jesus Christ, do not delay,
   But hasten our salvation;
   We often tremble on our way
   In fear and tribulation
   O hear and grant our fervent plea;
   Come, mighty judge, and set us free
   From death and ev'ry evil.

Text: Bartholomäus Ringwaldt, 1532–99; tr. Philip A. Peter, 1832–1919, alt. Public domain.

CHAPTER 5

RECASTING HEAVEN: THE NEW CREATION

Introduction

Then I saw a new heaven and a new earth, for the first heaven
and the first earth had passed away, and the sea was no more.
And I saw the holy city, new Jerusalem, coming down out of
heaven from God, prepared as a bride adorned for her husband.
And I heard a loud voice from the throne saying, "Behold, the
dwelling place of God is with man. He will dwell with them,
and they will be His people, and God Himself will be with
them as their God. He will wipe away every tear from their
eyes, and death shall be no more, neither shall there be mourning, nor crying, nor pain anymore, for the former things have
passed away. (Revelation 21:1–4)

In this chapter we will try to put a great mystery of the Christian faith into
human terms, namely heaven. What is heaven? Is it a place? Does it have a
location? Or are we trying to grasp something that isn't obtainable? Is it yet
another mystery of God that we can only imagine?

Here are a few ways people have described it:

- Heaven is filled with a vast array of color; it is not monochromatic.[100]
- It is not a place where one would ever be bored, as it allows each
  of us to be more than we have ever been before.
- It is a place where we are filled with a greater knowledge of reality
  and a much greater understanding of love.
- In many ways, heaven is the true understanding of reality.
- Heaven is free of pain, sin, death, and sorrow.

---

100   Varied shades of a single color.

- It is where everything exudes joy.
- It is always filled with the glorious light of Christ.

Most Christians are comforted by the idea of heaven being a place where they will dwell with God forever after death. Others consider heaven to be where Christ is, where He reigns and rules. Some believe heaven is where we are transformed into angels or we become something other than human. But the Scriptures do not describe or specifically tell us what heaven is.

Heaven is still one of the great mysteries of God. The famous hymn "I'm but a Stranger Here" (*LSB* 748) says that heaven is our home. All in all, these are not bad thoughts. But let's roll up our sleeves and see what the Bible actually says and what our Church Fathers,[101] Luther, and others have to say about heaven.

In this chapter we will try to put into our own words what the Bible proclaims about heaven. We'll discover some truths about heaven, but we will also break down—and hopefully, eliminate—some misconceptions.

QUESTIONS FOR DISCUSSION

Why does it matter or what difference does it make that we understand heaven?

Understanding heaven correctly might actually get one excited about what is yet to come. Rather than floating around on clouds, not doing much of anything, what about the idea of residing in a similar fashion as we are today, but without sin and death, and being continually in the presence of Jesus? False conclusions about heaven can turn the focus away from the only means of salvation: faith in Jesus Christ alone.

What impact might a proper understanding of heaven have on how we live our everyday life?

---

101 The Early Church Fathers fall into basically three categories. The Apostolic Fathers were contemporaries of the apostles and were probably taught by them. They carried on the rich traditions of the apostles. Examples of Apostolic Fathers would be Clement and Polycarp. The Ante-Nicene Church Fathers were the ones who came after the Apostolic Fathers but before the Council of Nicaea in AD 325. This group would include Justin Martyr and Irenaeus. The third group, the Post-Nicene Fathers, are those after the Council of Nicaea. Such Fathers include Augustine, Eusebius, and Jerome. The Church Fathers were the theologians of their day and were critical in determining the standard for what are today considered basic biblical teachings, such as understanding Christ's humanity and divinity, Baptism, the Eucharist, and understanding the Trinity. The period of the Church Fathers covers at least a thousand years after Christ's death.

There could be an amazing impact! What if the earth on which we now live, after being refined, becomes our eternal home? How might that affect the way we care for creation today? God has made us stewards of this amazing, yet groaning, creation. Imagine what it might be like if we cared for it now with an eternal picture of it in our minds.

Share with others your vision of heaven.

How were your ideas of heaven shaped or formed?

Biblical Understanding

For the most part, the Bible uses the word *heaven* to refer to two different things.[102] First, it is an expanse above, like the sky. In the account of the creation we read, "In the beginning, God created the heavens and the earth" (Genesis 1:1). Second, heaven is the dwelling place of God and His angels. When Abraham was about to offer his son Isaac as a sacrifice to God, we read, "The angel of the LORD called to him from heaven and said, 'Abraham, Abraham!' And he said, 'Here I am'" (22:11). Later, when King Solomon dedicated the temple, he prayed, "And listen to the plea of Your servant and of our people Israel, when they pray toward this place. And listen in heaven Your dwelling place, and when You hear, forgive" (1 Kings 8:30).

In many ways Mark combines these two concepts: "And when [Jesus] came up out of the water, immediately He saw the heavens being torn open and the Spirit descending on Him like a dove. And a voice came from heaven, 'You are My beloved Son; with You I am well pleased'" (Mark 1:10–11).

Here the heavens are rended open, the expanse of the sky is opened, and the Spirit of God descends from heaven and rests upon Jesus. It is all finally pulled together when we hear the voice of God coming down from the heavens. This text shows us both concepts of heaven: the heavens are the sky, or the expanse above, as in the creation text, but heaven is also the dwelling place of God. In this text we see the Spirit descending from heaven.

Forty days after His resurrection, Jesus ascended into heaven. "So then the Lord Jesus, after He had spoken to them, was taken up into heaven and sat

---

102   *Luther's Small Catechism with Explanation*, 225.

down at the right hand of God" (Mark 16:19). We see illustrated here the biblical explanation of heaven as a created thing of God and a place where God dwells.

There can be no doubt biblically that heaven is where God, in trinitarian fashion as Father, Son, and Holy Spirit, dwells. Heaven did not and could not exist before creation, for Genesis 1:1 tells us, "God created the heavens and the earth." He created heaven as a place for His creatures to dwell with Him.[103]

But we must not think of God as being contained within heaven. He fills all His creation (Jeremiah 23:24; Ephesians 1:23). But our human brains, our understanding, can't comprehend the vastness of God. Trying to comprehend the vastness of heaven is similar. It is ineffable, unfathomable, incomprehensible, yet it is a creation of our amazing Creator.

Heaven as a Metaphor

So how can or do we talk about heaven? We do it through human language, through our speech of what we know, and it is usually explained through metaphorical language.

A metaphor is a figure of speech, a phrase that is not used literally but rather to suggest a likeness. It can be used to represent or symbolize something else. A metaphor brings into view a reality that may not be attained through a literal interpretation. The Bible often speaks in metaphoric language. A good example of metaphoric language is when Jesus said, "I am the door of the sheep" (John 10:7). When people read this, they don't think of Jesus as a piece of wood. Rather, they realize that Jesus is the way we gain access to our Creator's presence. We enter through Christ into a true faith and through Him gain eternal life.

Another example of a metaphor is God's throne in heaven (Revelation 4:2). Some Christians interpret this literally instead of metaphorically and limit God to one place, thus excluding Him from all others places. But since Scripture indicates that God fills all His creation, the "throne of God" is more likely intended to be translated as a metaphor meaning God's sovereign ruling

---

103   This includes the angels and other spirit creatures invisible to sinful humans. These are included in the Nicene Creed's First Article, "I believe in one God, the Father Almighty, maker of heaven and earth and of all things visible and invisible."

presence throughout His creation. Understanding this as a metaphor does not limit God to one locality, but teaches us what Jesus means when He promises, "And behold, I am with you always, to the end of the age" (Matthew 28:20).

Heaven is a complex reality that God describes using metaphorical or figurative language to help us understand this reality. In fact, "not only is language about heaven metaphor: heaven is itself the metaphor of metaphors, for a metaphor opens to more and more meaning, and heaven is an unbordered meadow of meaning."[104]

The metaphors Scripture often uses to describe heaven include a garden, city, kingdom, and celestial sphere. Jesus most often refers to heaven as a kingdom or as the rule and reign of God. Let's look a bit more closely at the origins of these metaphors.

The metaphor of a garden is most often identified with its origin in the Hebrew Bible as the garden of earthly Paradise when the world first began. This would be seen as the original dwelling place of Adam, or the "enclosed garden." The idea of earthly paradise or a garden as a metaphor for heaven is closely linked to the springs or fountains beneath the throne of God. Symbolically, fountains and rivers bring forth life, and the idea of heaven portrays eternal life. Thus it becomes easy to see heaven as a garden.

The image of heaven as a city links powerfully with the image of heaven as a kingdom whose ruler is the Messiah, the King of Israel, the Anointed One. This, too, is found in the Bible.

The Jewish tradition has often linked heaven to the city of Jerusalem and to Mount Zion, a hill in Jerusalem just outside the old city, usually identified with the city of David and later the Temple Mount. Many rabbis have made a direct connection between the physical Jerusalem and the heavenly city. This heavenly city preexists the earthly city, which is merely a representation of its greater glory. But when Jerusalem fell in AD 70, rabbis moved away from this idea of it being the heavenly city.[105]

Humans have no way of knowing absolute truths about heaven, but the Bible provides us a few hints. Realize we cannot obtain a thorough analysis or picture of heaven from these passages, but we can create concepts or images

---

104   Russell, *A History of Heaven*, 9.

105   Russell, *A History of Heaven*, 14–15.

in our mind that provide us with a human concept of heaven. These concepts have been expressed in theology, art, poetry, liturgy, and narrative. So let's take a closer look at the concept of heaven beginning with the Bible. Later we will examine how the Church Fathers conceived of heaven and, finally, how Luther provided a concept of heaven.

The Bible and Heaven

How does the Bible talk about heaven? A tension seems to exist between understanding heaven as beyond the earth and at the same time part of the earth. Yet most would agree that heaven is usually understood as a sacred place.

Heaven is traditionally described as a place or as a part of the created world. "In the beginning, God created the heavens and the earth" (Genesis 1:1). The plural "heavens" indicates both the sky above us and the dwelling place of God, the angels, and the saints. Again, this heaven is a real place God created so creatures could dwell in His presence.

Let's start with what we do know. Scripture is very clear that Jesus is preparing a place for us. But Scripture also clearly states that God's kingdom will come to earth and that we, God's creatures, will be physically resurrected. What does Scripture say about this place as a familiar, physical, and tangible place?

The Bible is clear that heaven, which will one day be centered on the new earth, is real. Because of Jesus' ascension into heaven, many of us look to the clouds above and imagine heaven as an invisible place beyond. But one day we will simply look around us and see heaven—a world that is without sin, without death, suffering, or corruption. The image is difficult to grasp now, but when we get our first glimpse of the new heaven and the new earth at the resurrection of the dead we will see God face to face and delight in our heavenly home.

As we consider heaven from a scriptural standpoint, let's start with Colossians 3:1–3, where we learn to live as those who have been made alive in Christ: "If then you have been raised with Christ, seek the things that are above, where Christ is, seated at the right hand of God. Set your minds on things that are above, not on things that are on earth. For you have died, and your life is hidden with Christ in God." As Christians, our focus should be turned to our new life in Christ. With our focus there, our concept of our heavenly home begins to grow and expand. But this can be difficult when our minds are set on earth itself.

For those who trust in Christ, heaven will be their eternal home. For those who trust in themselves, hell will be their eternal home. As Jesus states in John 14:6, "I am the way, and the truth, and the life. No one comes to the Father except through Me." There is no middle ground once we die. We are either with Christ or we aren't.

What evidence does the Bible provide to fill out our picture of heaven? The texts of Isaiah 51:3, Ezekiel 36:35, and Revelation 22:1 provide the reader a glimpse of God's promise of restoration, the fulfillment of His promise for salvation, and a vision of the end times realized as a return to Eden, the garden of the Lord.

Isaiah 51:3 states, "For the LORD comforts Zion; He comforts all her waste places and makes her wilderness like Eden, her desert like the garden of the LORD; joy and gladness will be found in her, thanksgiving and the voice of song." Ezekiel 36:35 says this: "And they will say, 'This land that was desolate has become like the garden of Eden, and the waste and desolate and ruined cities are now fortified and inhabited.'" Revelation 22:1–2 describes heaven like so: "Then the angel showed me the river of the water of life, bright as crystal, flowing from the throne of God and of the Lamb through the middle of the street of the city; also, on either side of the river, the tree of life with its twelve kinds of fruit, yielding its fruit each month. The leaves of the tree were for the healing of the nations." Tying these three passages together, we have a vision of heaven.

The Book of Hebrews shows Christ's reign through the Church on earth as a copy of His reign in heaven. Hebrews 8:5 describes the construction of the tent of meeting and its furnishings: "They serve a copy and shadow of the heavenly things. For when Moses was about to erect the tent, he was instruct-ed by God, saying, 'See that you make everything according to the pattern that was shown you on the mountain.'" Again, in Hebrews 9:23–24, "Thus it was necessary for the copies of the heavenly things to be purified with these rites, but the heavenly things themselves with better sacrifices than these. For Christ has entered, not into holy places made with hands, which are copies of the true things, but into heaven itself, now to appear in the presence of God on our behalf."

When we see earthly things as copies of heavenly things, we begin to abandon the idea that something that exists in one realm can't exist in the other. In other words, we need to stop thinking of earth and heaven as opposites and instead see them as overlapping circles that share certain commonalities. C. S. Lewis proposed a similar view. He asked one to consider the hills and valleys of heaven to be not so much a copy of or substitute for the genuine article, but instead more as a diamond might be compared to coal or the flower to the root.[106]

Scripture provides us with puzzle pieces, if you will, to help us piece together a vision or concept of heaven. For example, in Hebrews 11:10 and 13:14, we are told that heaven is a city whose builder and maker is God, and it is a city that we will seek. Heaven is also described as a country. Look at Hebrews 11:16: "But as it is, they desire a better country, that is, a heavenly one."

It becomes helpful at this point to turn our focus toward the new heavens and new earth. Because the earth we know now has been badly damaged by our sin, we turn our thoughts and minds to the world as it was before to imagine what it will be in the future. That will be our eternal home.

When we see beautiful flowers, roaring waterfalls, or amazing sunsets, we should yearn for our eternal home because these provide us with glimpses of our heavenly home that is yet to come. We should not close our eyes to the scarred wonder of creation around us but take it all in and try to imagine it without sin, corruption, or death. In those moments we are getting a brief glimpse of the new earth to come.

Earth matters, our bodies matter, and all of creation matters—first, because God created it all and, second, because He will return and redeem it all. With this in mind, let's consider how our Church Fathers and Luther himself envisioned heaven.

The Church Fathers and Luther on Heaven

Since the second century, Christian writers have sought a more figurative way for understanding heaven. They asked, What is heaven? Does it exist?

---

106   C. S. Lewis, *Letters to Malcolm: Chiefly on Prayer* (New York: Harcourt Brace Jovanovich, 1963), 84.

And if it does exist, how are we to define it? In the second century, philosophy and theology were deeply intertwined, so many of the thoughts about heaven that have come down to us carry traces and implications connected to philosophy.

CYPRIAN

Cyprian, a bishop of Carthage who lived AD 210–49, became a notable Christian writer who considered heaven to be much like a port, a native land. It was a meeting place where saints, prophets, apostles, martyrs, and all our loved ones will once again meet to share eternity. For him, heaven meant being with Christ forever. But he also saw heaven as our common homeland and taught that we would be with all our friends, our relatives, and everyone who ever loved God.[107]

LACTANTIUS

Lactantius is another early Christian author and adviser who lived AD 240–320. He was a guide of religious policy to the Christian Roman emperor Constantine I. He also considered heaven as a place and believed that in heaven, we will remember our entire earthly life. But this teaching raised many unanswered questions: Do we remember the pain that went with all these memories? If we remember the pain, are we also able to see God's amazing forgiveness washed over us?

Like other Fathers, Lactantius explored heaven's landscape. In a poem that is usually attributed to Lactantius, "De Ave Phoenicea (The Phoenix)," he describes not only earthly paradise but also Christ's resurrection and the bodily resurrection of all believers. The poem begins by depicting the Garden of Eden as Paradise. It is a beautiful garden in the "east," meant only for those who believe in Christ. And in this "new" land it emits nothing but sweet smells as the garden is abundantly filled with blooming foliage that never dies.

In paradise, there is no death, no tears, no sickness or misery. Its weather is always mild, the sun never too hot, with no need for rain or snow. The phoenix itself becomes the symbol for Christ who resides in the garden, this "new creation." At one point, the poem talks about believers being joined in flight

---

107   Russell, *A History of Heaven*, 65.

with Christ, souls together with body, to soar with abundant joy above the heavenly city.

Like Lactantius, many theologians and philosophers of this time used metaphoric language to put images to their concept of heaven. Many of the early writers taught and believed that heaven was a place where all God's people, the Jews of the Old Covenant and the baptized Christians, joined together in the eternal light of God. There was much controversy over who this might involve, but most agreed Christ's martyrs were included along with all baptized Christians. In the end, heaven was simply seen as a place where God's people meet for eternity.

TERTULLIAN

Tertullian, who lived between AD 155 and AD 240, was a bit more unorthodox in his thinking about heaven, even though he later became a cornerstone theologian of the Latin Fathers and greatly influenced the Church's theology in both the East and West. Tertullian had a more millennial understanding of heaven. He believed that at the end time, the blessed will rise in their bodies and enjoy a thousand-year reign with Christ in the New Jerusalem rebuilt by God on earth. After this reign, the saved will be removed from heaven and will take on the substance of angels. This interpretation of Revelation was rejected in the fifth century, but it still can be found among Christians today.[108]

By the third century, the language of heaven was refocused toward understanding heaven as paradise. Tertullian was the first to speak this way. He wrote one of the first books that we know of that was devoted to paradise, *On Paradise*. In his book, which unfortunately has been lost, Tertullian imagines paradise much as Scripture describes, with the original Paradise being transformed or re-created into a celestial paradise where the martyrs and all the baptized will live eternally.

EPHRAIM OF SYRIA

Ephraim of Syria (also known as St. Ephraem or Ephrem, AD 306–73) wrote a variety of poems, hymns, and sermons to edify the Church in troubled times. He made his mark in connecting earthly paradise with the Church and

---

108   Ibid., 67.

ultimately with celestial paradise. He believed that paradise is not a specific location; rather, it is everywhere. When you die, you don't "go to heaven"; instead, you come to realize that heaven is everywhere and has always existed all around you. He also rightly claimed that although our bodies rot in the grave, God will raise them miraculously, and our present bodies will be glorified.

AMBROSE OF MILAN

Ambrose, the bishop of Milan, who lived AD 337–97 and wrote the treatise *On Paradise*, identified paradise directly with the heavenly Jerusalem. (Interesting note: Ambrose was one of the original doctors of the Church.) Ambrose widened the theological distinction between the imagery of the celestial and earthly paradise. For Ambrose, earthly paradise is the place where humans, according to the body, are fully human, whereas in celestial paradise, humans will "take on" additional attributes according to the image of God, becoming even more fully human. In heaven, separation no longer exists, either from our loved ones or, more important, from Christ Himself. We, His children, will be yoked to Him forever. Here we inch a bit closer to a biblical understanding of heaven.

THE CAPPADOCIANS

The Eastern Church, much like the Western, did not lack for theological speculation about heaven or paradise. The most well known speculations in this regard are those of the Cappadocians Gregory of Nazianzus, Basil the Great, and Gregory of Nyssa. They taught that even though we may never truly understand the divine essence of God and eternity within the heavenly realm, we will be satisfied, for there will be no need to completely comprehend all that is around us.

AUGUSTINE

Augustine of Hippo, one of the greatest influences and writers of the Western Church, took the reality of heaven, conceived of as a place, and recast it toward an understanding of Christ Himself. Augustine started by teaching that salvation is a journey or pilgrimage in which we all travel to our final destination, the heavenly Jerusalem. And where does that journey begin? At our Baptism, of course, and it continues until we reach "heaven."

But for Augustine, to be fully in heaven is to fully be in Christ Himself. When we die—and all will die—God Himself in Christ becomes the place to which we go. And because God is eternal, we enter eternity in Him. Augustine moved beyond the idea of eternity as endless time and toward the idea of "a transcendent eternity" where eternity is ever present, ever before us. For Augustine, eternity was celestial paradise, the paradise of all paradises ever imagined.[109] This celestial paradise, when seen in contrast to earthly paradise, is both eternal and eschatological. "It is the fulfillment at the end of time, the sabbath of sabbaths, an eighth day of creation when we shall 'rest and see, see and love, love and praise.'"[110]

Augustine painted his vision of heaven in his famous work *The City of God*. In this work he turned his sight upward to a kingdom that far surpasses all human understanding. And in his *Confessions*, he insisted that one is not able to rest until one rests in God. For Augustine, God and heaven are one and the same. It's not a place but a reality. Heaven is God within us as well as surrounding us. It's the ultimate reality and completeness of our being whole and in union with God. It is true blessedness and joy.

MARTIN LUTHER

In his great Reformation style, Martin Luther talks about heaven as simply and always a gift of the grace of God in Christ Jesus. He also refers to heaven as a glory that will be—and is now—revealed in us. This, I believe, points us right back to Luther seeing heaven as pure grace received both now and in the future, and that grace is Christ alone. In Christ, we have everything we will ever need. In Christ alone we find our salvation, our hope, our life, and our future life in paradise.

Today, heaven is revealed and realized in Christ—in His incarnation, death, burial, resurrection, ascension, and in His coming again. When we take our eyes off Jesus, we miss the opening of heaven for all mankind. Today we live in the in-between; we hear and see echoes of Eden while approaching the new earth.

---

109   Ibid., 85.

110   Ibid.

Taking Our Eyes Off Christ

Don't take your eyes off Jesus, because in Jesus, heaven's reality is revealed. How is it revealed? Jesus, in His death and dying, opens realities unseen. We've heard over and over in sermons that Jesus died for our sins. This is an amazingly true statement, but Jesus did so much more when He died. In His death, He broke the chains of Satan; He crushed the serpent's head. By giving Himself up to death He freed us from fearing death.

Jesus did not only die; He was also buried. In first-century Jerusalem, once the body was dead, it was laid out in a rock-hewn tomb, either in a *niche* (a shaft cut as deep as a body) or on an *arcosolium* (a bench or shelf cut out of the wall of the tomb). In Jesus' case, He was laid in a new tomb near the place of His death (John 19:41). Because it was the Jewish day of preparation, the day before the Sabbath, they were only able to give Jesus' body a preliminary anointing: "Nicodemus also, who earlier had come to Jesus by night, came bringing a mixture of myrrh and aloes, about seventy-five pounds in weight. So they took the body of Jesus and bound it in linen cloths with the spices" (John 19:39–40). "Then, when the Sabbath was past, Mary Magdalene, Mary the mother of James, and Salome bought spices, so that they might go and anoint Him" (Mark 16:1).

On the morning of that first day of the week, the women came to the tomb only to find Jesus' body missing. Yet, throughout Jesus' ministry, He had told His disciples and others that after His death, He would rise (Matthew 16:21; 17:22–23; 20:18–19; 26:32; 27:63; Mark 8:31; 9:9–10; 9:31; 10:34; 14:28; Luke 18:33; 24:6–7; John 2:19).

A heavenly messenger testified to the women that Jesus had risen from the dead (see Matthew 28:1, 5–6; Mark 16:1, 5–6; Luke 24:1–5). Luke's account includes the following declaration from this messenger: "Why do you seek the living among the dead?" (v. 5). Jesus had been raised from the dead, and each Gospel account provides multiple witnesses to the fact that Jesus now lived with a physical, tangible body.

What does this mean for us? In Revelation 2:8, Jesus gives us comfort through John's letter to the Church in Smyrna: "The words of the first and the last, who died and came to life" (Revelation 2:8). In His death and burial, Jesus has removed the fear and sting of the grave by dying and lying in the tomb. We no longer fear death, because He has risen victoriously from the grave and now reigns. Yet, Jesus does not stop there. Near His empty tomb He made another bold statement to Mary Magdalene: "Do not cling to Me, for I have not yet ascended to the Father; but go to My brothers and say to them, 'I am ascending to My Father and your Father, to My God and your God'" (John 20:17).

In His incarnation, Christ came from heaven to earth to fulfill His mission on earth. In His ascension, He returned to heaven to take His seat at the right hand of the Father. And when He comes again, when He returns to earth, He will make all things new and heaven will be revealed in Him once again. This new heaven will be "what no eye has seen, nor ear heard, nor the heart of man imagined, what God has prepared for those who love Him" (1 Corinthians 2:9). What has God prepared for those who love Him? What will we see? What will we hear? What will our hearts conceive?

[God says,] "For behold, I create new heavens and a new earth." (Isaiah 65:17)

"For as the new heavens and the new earth that I make shall remain before Me, says the LORD, so shall your offspring and your name remain." (Isaiah 66:22)

But according to His promise we are waiting for new heavens and a new earth in which righteousness dwells. (2 Peter 3:13)

Then I saw a new heaven and a new earth, for the first heaven and the first earth had passed away. (Revelation 21:1)

I think it is safe to say that today we live in that heavenly reality. We say it each time we recite in the Lord's Prayer, "Thy will be done, on earth as it is in heaven." Yes, the focus here is God's will in our lives, but we ask that will to be done on earth as it is in heaven, providing a direct correlation between earth and heaven and providing a glimpse of heaven's reality. Preparation for heaven's reality begins here on earth.

In the New Testament, Mark's Gospel literally opens and closes with the rending of the heavens.[111] The heavens are split open in Jesus' Baptism in Mark 1:10, and the curtain of the temple splits in 15:38. Why is this important? Because here, not only does Jesus' death reveal who He is and what He

---

111   James Voelz, *Mark 1:1–8:26*, Concordia Commentary (St. Louis: Concordia, 2013).

brings to earth, but He also reveals eternal life to us.

Throughout the New Testament, Jesus' emphasis on the parables of the kingdom of heaven lead us to believe that there was something to be learned both now while living in God's earthly creation and in the age to come. This is the "now and not yet" tension we live in as Christians. Now, today, we live in God's good but groaning creation, and this good creation is a foretaste of what is to come. Christ in His coming prepares us now for what will come, for that which has been prepared for us. The "now" and the "not yet" collide. The words of 1 Peter 1:3–5 help us to focus on that which has been prepared for us:

> Blessed be the God and Father of our Lord Jesus Christ!
> According to His great mercy, He has caused us to be born
> again to a living hope through the resurrection of Jesus
> Christ from the dead, to an inheritance that is imperishable,
> undefiled, and unfading, kept in heaven for you, who by
> God's power are being guarded through faith for a salvation
> ready to be revealed in the last time.

Through Christ's resurrection we have inherited eternal life in Him. We have been made righteous in Him. We have hope in Him. This text leads us to rejoice in what God has done and what He intends to do for His people. It provides us a picture of our inheritance and reveals to us the salvation promised in Old Testament prophecy. The redemption of heaven and earth, the promised eschatological future, is secure, even in the present.

In order to understand heaven today, in our present state, we need to take a closer look at eternity. In Ecclesiastes 3, specifically verse 11, God has put eternity in man's mind. Verses 1–11 provide us with a vision of that eternity in the "now" and the "not yet":

> For everything there is a season, and a time for every matter un-
> der heaven: a time to be born, and a time to die; a time to plant,
> and a time to pluck up what is planted; a time to kill, and a time
> to heal; a time to break down, and a time to build up; a time to
> weep, and a time to laugh; a time to mourn, and a time to dance;
> a time to cast away stones, and a time to gather stones together; a
> time to embrace, and a time to refrain from embracing; a time to

seek, and a time to lose; a time to keep, and a time to cast away; a time to tear, and a time to sew; a time to keep silence, and a time to speak; a time to love, and a time to hate; a time for war, and a time for peace. What gain has the worker from his toil? I have seen the business that God has given to the children of man to be busy with. He has made everything beautiful in its time. Also, He has put eternity into man's heart, yet so that he cannot find out what God has done from the beginning to the end.

God has put eternity into man's heart. This, I believe, provides for us a foretaste of what will come to those in Christ in eternity. Heaven is not a distraction from earth; rather, it teaches us how to live here and now. Heaven and earth, time and eternity, are brought together in Christ Jesus.

QUESTIONS FOR DISCUSSION

How does trusting in Christ provide us with a template for understanding eternity?

When we focus on Christ Jesus, our future is more clearly defined. Knowing that you will be in the presence of Christ eternally changes your vision. In some ways, it doesn't matter where we are or when we die because we have been promised a life without pain, without death, without a lot of what makes life difficult now.

What words of Christ direct us to find shelter and hope in Him alone?

"I am the way, and the truth" (John 14:6). "Today you will be with Me in paradise" (Luke 23:43). "I am with you always, to the end of the age" (Matthew 28:20). "Be still, and know that I am God. I will be exalted among the nations, I will be exalted in the earth!" (Psalm 46:10). There are many, many others. Think of another passage that turns your focus to Christ alone.

What promises can you recount that provide you with a glimpse of heaven on earth?

Understanding Eternity to Understand Heaven

In order to better understand heaven, it is important to get a better understanding of what we mean when we talk about eternity. Do eternity and heaven coexist? When we speak of heaven, are we also speaking of eternity?

Usually, eternity is understood as having to do with the concept of time, of being infinite, without limit, or having unending time. It has also been understood as timelessness. But eternity is not timelessness. Instead, all time is perfected in eternity. It is the fullness of time. This is hard to conceive of because we put boundaries on time—and yet eternity has no boundaries.

The fullness of time is not found only in Christ's first coming, but includes His second coming, which is the consummation of time. Eternity redeems time and can't be put on a timeline.

Think of it this way. Consider time as a line. You can mark a specific point on that line, but the point doesn't stop the line; it is only one of many points on the line. The point marks time, but there is no true reality to that point in time. You see, eternity is present in time, yet it is neither a part of time nor apart from time.[112]

Let's try to simplify this. Eternity is a concept that most of us have difficulty fully comprehending. Let's start with God. I think we can all agree that God exists outside the realm of time. Yet, He sent His Son, Jesus, into the realm of time, at His perfect time, to accomplish His plan. Therefore, the dimension of time does not and cannot limit God. God, through His Son, enters time and introduces eternity to the world, or better yet, eternal life—a slightly easier concept to ponder.

The term *eternal life* is not found in the Bible until Jesus becomes incarnate and enters time. The Book of John tells us not only what eternal life is but who can receive eternity. John 17:3 says, "And this is eternal life, that they know You, the only true God, and Jesus Christ whom You have sent." "For God so loved the world, that He gave His only Son, that whoever believes in Him should not perish but have eternal life" (John 3:16). "Truly, truly, I say to you, whoever hears My word and believes Him who sent Me has eternal life" (John 5:24). "For this is the will of My Father, that everyone who looks on the Son and believes in Him should have eternal life, and I will raise Him up on the last day" (John 6:40). Here, not only are we told where eternal life comes from, but we are also reminded that with eternal life comes the resurrection of the body.

---

112   Peter Kreeft, *Everything You Ever Wanted to Know about Heaven* (San Francisco: Ignatius Press, 1990), 175.

Paul helps us pull together this same concept of eternal life and the raising of our bodies on the Last Day:

> So we do not lose heart. Though our outer self is wasting away, our inner self is being renewed day by day. For this light momentary affliction is preparing for us an eternal weight of glory beyond all comparison, as we look not to the things that are seen but to the things that are unseen. For the things that are seen are transient, but the things that are unseen are eternal. For we know that if the tent that is our earthly home is destroyed, we have a building from God, a house not made with hands, eternal in the heavens. (2 Corinthians 4:16–5:1)

God alone can transform time. He did this when Jesus became human and entered time. He also transformed our time. By faith, eternal life is already our present possession.

No one ever truly has enough time. But if we can grasp that all time is present in eternity, then one also knows that if you want more time, you must come to the One who keeps all time: "To the Eternal One, the Lord of time. You must give Him your time, your few loaves and fishes, and He will multiply them miraculously. He is time's keeper and time's dispenser; He is the 'housekeeper who brings out of His storeroom things both new and old.'"[113] (See Matthew 13:52.)

Heaven is life in Christ. Christ came to establish His kingdom, "the Kingdom of Heaven on earth, to begin eternal life in time, to put divinity in humanity, first in Christ and then in the Christian, first in the Head and then throughout His Body."[114] (See John 1:12; 1 Corinthians 15:20, 23.)

Heaven Recast toward the New Creation

If eternal life is found in Christ, then heaven is found in eternity. When we speak of heaven biblically the verb changes from past or future to the present tense: "Behold, I am making all things new" (Revelation 21:5). This is God's

---

113   Ibid., 170.

114   Ibid., 176.

redemptive plan. This plan is already in action.

It is a present reality. Christ's resurrection turns us, His children, toward the heavenly realm of eternal life now in this life. We live in God's reality of hope now. We live in heaven on earth now, in God's new creation, and we look forward to the completion of His work in the "new heaven and new earth."

We don't look toward heaven for eternity; instead, we look to the new heavens and new earth because that hope has already come in the life of Jesus of Nazareth. In this life we have already passed from death to life, and each week we proclaim this reality through the recitation of the creeds when we confess that we believe in "the resurrection of the body."

Let's step back just a bit and consider this basic question: What is it about the resurrection of Jesus that changes that understanding? What is it about the resurrection that provides us with a new template for recasting a new vision of heaven?

I am guessing that many of you picture heaven in a similar way to a popular book by Maria Shriver called *What's Heaven?*[115] The book, written for children, provides a visual interpretation of Shriver's idea of heaven. The pages are filled with pictures of fluffy clouds and messages like ones we hear all the time:

> Heaven is where God lives.

> Heaven is filled with lots of gold and jewels and unlimited resources.

> Heaven is soft clouds and hours of playing beautiful music.

> Heaven is where our loved ones who went before us look down upon us and watch over us until we join them.

> Heaven is the place you go when you die if you have been good.

> Heaven is where you become an angel, receive your wings, and sit on the clouds.

Does this sound familiar? I would guess millions of people across the Western world, Christians and non-Christians alike, believe this to be at least one vision of heaven, if not a total vision of heaven.

---

115   Maria Shriver, *What's Heaven?* (New York: St. Martin's Press, 2007).

But is this how the Bible speaks of heaven? Not at all. In fact, there is very little in the Bible about "going to heaven when you die." When the Bible speaks of "God's kingdom," it is not talking about a place people go when they die or a place to escape from this world to the next; it is talking about the rule and reign of God coming here on earth, as it is in heaven. Once again we are reminded of the language of the Lord's Prayer, "on earth as it is in heaven."

As we begin to recast the old vision of heaven, we need to keep two vital points at the forefront of our thinking. First, Christ's resurrection changed and continues to change everything. And second, heaven is a complex reality that we experience now, with and in Christ, but we will experience it in the fullest and most complete sense following the resurrection on the last day. Heaven is a present-day reality.

Whether we translate *heaven* as "the kingdom of God," "the kingdom of heaven," or "the reign and rule of God," all three are present-day realities. All three refer to now. God's reign and rule began when Jesus' ministry on earth began: "The time is fulfilled, and the kingdom of God is at hand" (Mark 1:15). This reality is also an eschatological reality.

Let's take a look at the Book of Revelation, specifically chapters 4–5. Here we see a vision of our present heavenly reality—as N. T. Wright would call it, "the heavenly dimension of our present life."[116] He describes this heavenly dimension: "Heaven, in the Bible, is not a future destiny but the other, hidden dimension of our ordinary life—God's dimension, if you like. God made heaven and earth; at the last He will remake both and join them together forever. And when we come to the picture of the actual end in Revelation 21–22, we find not ransomed souls making their way to a disembodied heaven but rather the new Jerusalem coming down from heaven to earth, uniting the two in a lasting embrace."[117]

Heaven is neither the same as nor different from earth but rather analogous to it. Better yet, earth is analogous to heaven; earth is heaven's image. Heaven transforms earthly things. "Earth is neither continued nor removed but *aufgehoben*, taken up, perfected and consummated."[118] God does not give up on

---

116 N. T. Wright, *Surprised by Hope: Rethinking Heaven, the Resurrection and the Mission of the Church* (New York: HarperOne, 2008), 19.

117 Ibid.

118 Kreeft, *Everything You Ever Wanted to Know*, 151–52.

His original creation. Hear the biblical vocabulary that makes this a reality: "Reconcile." "Renew." "Redeem." "Recover." "Regenerate." "Resurrect." You get the picture. Each of these words begin with the prefix *re-*, suggesting a return to that which was originally created. Christ not only restores us; He also restores His creation to what it was intended to be.

This, too, is the language of Revelation. Dr. Louis A. Brighton, who was a professor at Concordia Seminary, St. Louis, describes it like this in his commentary on Revelation: "Here in Rev 21:1 John sees 'a new heaven and new earth' which take the place of 'the first heaven and the first earth.'"[119] There is a coming down of the new heaven and new earth. Brighton also speaks of two extrabiblical Jewish writings: "According to 1 Enoch[120] 45:4–6 the Lord declares that on the day of judgment he will 'transform the earth and make it a blessing.' . . . And 1 Enoch 91:16–17 promises that 'the first heaven shall depart and pass away,' and 'a new heaven shall appear.' . . . In 4 Ezra[121] 7:75, 88–99 a reference is made about God's people at rest in death until God renews the creation."[122]

Brighton reflects on Irenaeus's writing *Against Heresies*, 5.36.1, where Irenaeus explicitly compares and holds together the resurrected body of man with the new heaven and new earth when he writes, "As man is new in the resurrection, so there will be a new heaven and a new earth, and in this new heaven and earth resurrected man will remain."[123]

Brighton then makes a direct correlation between this new heaven and new earth and the new Jerusalem in Revelation: "the holy city, new Jerusalem, coming down out of heaven from God" (Revelation 21:2). This new Jerusalem is not a replica of the old Jerusalem restored; instead it is God's city, a city He created, a city He built, a city where God dwells, and a city that comes down

---

119   Louis A. Brighton, *Revelation*, Concordia Commentary (St. Louis: Concordia Publishing House, 1990), 593.

120   Enoch is a compilation of at least five Jewish writings dating approximately three centuries before the birth of Christ. Although classified among the Old Testament Pseudepigrapha they are not part of the Christian biblical canon. Today these writings provide us with historical evidence of Jewish thought and beliefs during this period.

121   The Book of Ezra can be found in the Hebrew Bible and traditionally was considered, along with Chronicles and Nehemiah, to be the second group of historical books, which contained some duplication but extended the "Deuteronomic" history that began with Joshua and ended with Kings. The book 4 Ezra is dated in the late first century AD and is also considered a pseudepigrapha like 1 Enoch.

122   Brighton, *Revelation*, 592.

123   Ibid.

to God's people to remain forever.

Finally, Brighton reflects on Revelation 21:3–4, where he makes a direct connection between the tabernacle of God in the Old Testament, the new heaven and new earth, and all God's people. In the Old Testament, the tabernacle of God was always present among God's people; *tabernacle* means "to dwell with, to be in the midst of." As the people of Israel moved through the wilderness, the tabernacle moved with them in their midst. "Behold, the dwelling place of God [the tabernacle] is with man. He will dwell with them, and they will be His people, and God Himself will be with them as their God" (Revelation 21:3). Brighton uses the word *tabernacle* to describe Christ's coming, the gracious and glorious presence of Christ with His people in the new heaven and the new earth. Christ comes to us, just as the new heaven and the new earth come to us. They come as the gift of God's promise. As Luther stated, it is pure grace.

This returns us to not taking our eyes off Jesus or His resurrection, because in Christ's resurrection, in this hope and reality, we find answers to the questions of heaven. "Today you will be with Me in paradise" does not speak to some disembodied spirit life after death, but refers instead to new bodily life, "the life *after* life after death."[124] This is the life we presently live in. Bodily life is as always a gift of God's grace and His love. Why new bodies? Wright surmises (correctly, I believe):

> The purpose of this new body will be to rule wisely over God's new world. Forget those images about lounging around playing harps. There will be work to do and we shall relish doing it. All the skills and talents we have to put to God's service in this present life—and perhaps too the interests and likings we gave up because they conflicted with our vocation—will be enhanced and ennobled and given back to us to be exercised in his glory. This is perhaps the most mysterious, and least explored, aspect of the resurrection life. . . . The biblical view of God's future is of the renewal of the entire cosmos, there will be plenty to be done. . . . The garden will need to be tended once more and the animals renamed.[125]

---

124   Wright, *Surprised by Hope*, 151.

125   Ibid., 161.

Here Wright not only provides us with his image of how God transforms our bodies to serve Him in the new creation but also helps point us toward thinking about our resurrected body as a reality in this life, now! This vision of the new heaven and new earth transforms the life we live each day here on earth even as it addresses how our resurrected bodies will be used to serve God and His creation eternally in the new heaven and new earth.

Conclusion

How can we use human language to define or better understand heaven? This chapter has shown us that heaven is not a place we long for while we live this life on earth. Heaven is not our distant home; earth is our home. It's not a destination point we arrive at once we die, and it certainly is not a place where our loved ones are looking down upon us until we die and join them.

Heaven, eternity, is found in Christ. It is where Christ is. Heaven is made alive in Christ. If we truly believe that Christ was raised from the dead, then our reality of life after life after death, our reality of heaven and eternity, are all caught up in Jesus. When Jesus comes again in His glory, He will bring with Him the New Jerusalem, the new heavens and new earth, the life of eternity.

We have spent many pages trying to metaphorically explain heaven, but the best way to grasp it is simply to turn to Jesus, the source of truth and life. In Christ, eternity becomes a reality. In Christ, we are made new. In Christ, we are transformed. He will raise our body to new life, to a new heaven and new earth, and we will live with Him eternally.

This chapter has not taken the mystery out of heaven. Heaven is still an amazing mystery. We really can't be sure what heaven will look like. We can't be sure what will be there—plants, animals, and the like. But if we consider the Garden of Eden from Genesis 1 and 2 before the fall, if we stop to look at God's amazing creation today, the colors, the magnificent landscapes (minus, of course, the scars of sin), we might have a pretty good idea.

As the physical heavens today declare God's glory (Psalm 19:1–2), so, too, will His glory be abundantly clear and on even greater display when creation is redeemed. "All the earth shall be filled with the glory of the LORD" (Numbers 14:21). God promises that on this new earth, "the glory of the LORD shall be revealed, and all flesh shall see it together" (Isaiah 40:5).

The Bridegroom Soon Will Call Us

1. The Bridegroom soon will call us,
   "Come to the wedding feast."
   May slumber not befall us
   Nor watchfulness decrease.
   May all our lamps be burning
   With oil enough and more
   That we, with Him returning,
   May find an open door!

2. There shall we see in glory
   Our dear Redeemer's face;
   The long-awaited story
   Of heav'nly joy takes place:
   The patriarchs shall meet us,
   The prophets' holy band;
   Apostles, martyrs greet us
   In that celestial land.

3. There God shall from all evil
   Forever make us free,
   From sin and from the devil,
   From all adversity,
   From sickness, pain, and sadness,
   From troubles, cares, and fears,
   And grant us heav'nly gladness
   And wipe away our tears.

4. In that fair home shall never
   Be silent music's voice;
   With hearts and lips forever

We shall in God rejoice,

While angel hosts are raising

With saints from great to least

A mighty hymn for praising

The Giver of the feast.

Text: Johann Walter, 1496–1570; tr. F. Samuel Janzow, 1913–2001, st. 1; tr. Matthias Loy, 1828–1915, sts. 2–4, alt. St. 1 © 1982 Concordia Publishing House; sts. 2–4 public domain.

CHAPTER 6

BODILY LIFE
IN GOD'S HEAVENLY CREATION

Introduction

For behold, I create new heavens and a new earth, and the
former things shall not be remembered or come into mind. But
be glad and rejoice forever in that which I create; for behold,
I create Jerusalem to be a joy, and her people to be a gladness.
I will rejoice in Jerusalem and be glad in My people; no more
shall be heard in it the sound of weeping and the cry of distress.
(Isaiah 65:17–19)

Living in the Kingdom of God on the New Earth

For I consider that the sufferings of this present time are not
worth comparing with the glory that is to be revealed to us. For
the creation waits with eager longing for the revealing of the sons
of God. For the creation was subjected to futility, not willingly,
but because of Him who subjected it, in hope that the creation
itself will be set free from its bondage to corruption and obtain the
freedom of the glory of the children of God. For we know that the
whole creation has been groaning together in the pains of child-
birth until now. And not only the creation, but we ourselves, who
have the firstfruits of the Spirit, groan inwardly as we wait eagerly
for adoption as sons, the redemption of our bodies. For in this
hope we were saved. Now hope that is seen is not hope. For who
hopes for what he sees? But if we hope for what we do not see, we
wait for it with patience. (Romans 8:18–25)

Paul's words to the Christians in Rome capture well the hope of those who treasure the promise of the resurrection: not only will the children of God be set free from bondage, but so will the earth and the whole creation obtain the glory of the children of God. The creation, including our planet, lives in that hope as well and will be transformed.[126] This transformed earth will be the dwelling place of the saints, those who have "washed their robes and made them white in the blood of the Lamb" (Revelation 7:14). It will also be the place to which God brings heaven, His dwelling place, when He descends through and in His Son, Jesus Christ, upon the earth.

As we saw in the last chapter, our traditional understanding of heaven as the place where our resurrected bodies (not just disembodied souls) go for eternity must be biblically redirected. We will dwell on the new earth, the old fallen earth put to death and raised to new life, as the human creatures who participate in the wholeness of life that the Trinity originally intended for us. Ever since Christ's ascension into heaven, God has been preparing in heaven the gift of a new earth that He will reveal at Christ's return. And the dwelling and throne of God, what the Bible calls "heaven" or "the heavenly city," will also be unveiled on this new earth.

> Then I saw a new heaven and a new earth, for the first heaven
> and the first earth had passed away, and the sea was no more.
> And I saw the holy city, new Jerusalem, coming down out of
> heaven from God, prepared as a bride adorned for her husband.
> (Revelation 21:1–2)

All believers in Christ will live on the new earth with God in Christ dwelling with us. Sound familiar? It's the restoration of paradise (Genesis 2:8). This is the kingdom of God, God's rule in Christ from heaven now revealed on the renewed and restored earth. That is paradise. That is heaven. That is where we will live eternally in the bodies that the Creator made and gave to us.

---

126 Francis Pieper, in volume 3 of his *Christian Dogmatics* (St. Louis: Concordia Publishing House, 1953), 543, notes that various Lutheran theologians have held the opinion that either the old creation will be transformed into the new creation or it will be annihilated and a completely new creation spring forth. He notes that this is a theological opinion, not a doctrinal matter. I think Romans 8 points toward a transformation that includes an actual dying of the planet, but not necessarily a complete annihilation/destruction. The old planet dies, and out of the dead planet a new planet comes to life, just as what happened in Christ's death and resurrection. His body was not annihilated but was transformed through death. A visual metaphor that might be helpful for this transformation is the death and transformation of the beast in *Beauty and the Beast*, back into the prince that he was before he was cursed. His beastly body is not annihilated, but through his death his body is transformed from its beastly character to its human and princely character.

QUESTIONS FOR DISCUSSION

How does the redirected vision of heaven reorient your understanding of paradise?

This reoriented vision places the Son of God, Jesus Christ, and God's kingdom squarely at the center of paradise. It also helps us to see that God created us to dwell on the earth, in this case the earth perfected and made whole. We are bodily creatures and God created us to dwell in a physical place, a renewed earth with heaven in the middle of it.

If our eternal home will be on an earthly paradise, then what is its most important characteristic?

The most important characteristic of the earthly paradise, for which we long, is that the crucified and living Lord, the Word of God the Father, will by the Spirit breathe eternal life into everything. He will be its life, its foundation, its solidity, its light, its living water, its brilliance, its beauty, and its glory. It will be an earthly paradise because everything will receive eternal life from the tree, Christ Jesus, who is in the middle of the renewed earth and in relationship to everyone and everything in it.

Our Dwelling Place: The Kingdom of God on the New Earth

The resurrected body is *not* about going to heaven, at least not heaven as we often conceive of it. It is about living in our resurrected body on earth with heaven having come down to earth. Since heaven is God's realm (or temple, or sanctuary) and God's throne room, it is also the place where God accomplishes His will before the final days and the return of Christ.[127] It is this very thing for which we pray in the Lord's Prayer: "Your kingdom come, Your will be done, on earth as it is in heaven" (Matthew 6:10). The prayer presumes that God's will is done *in heaven*, that His rule is established *in heaven*. We are praying for His will and reign to be established *on the earth*. That will only be fully realized when He comes again. Luther's explanation to the Second Petition of the Lord's Prayer, "Thy kingdom come," expresses the same idea:

---

127   I am dependent upon the thoughts of J. Richard Middleton in describing the nature of heaven. See J. Richard Middleton, *A New Heaven and a New Earth: Reclaiming Biblical Eschatology* (Grand Rapids, MI: Baker Academic, 2014), 71–73.

The kingdom of God certainly comes by itself without our prayer, but we pray in this petition that it may come to us also. *How does God's kingdom come?* God's kingdom comes when our heavenly Father gives us His Holy Spirit, so that by His grace we believe His holy Word and lead godly lives here in time and *there in eternity* [emphasis added].[128]

We will lead godly lives on the transformed earth in the presence of God's kingdom eternally. Jesus makes just this promise in the Beatitudes in Matthew 5:5 when He says, "Blessed are the meek, for they shall inherit the earth." We don't inherit heaven as some spiritualized, nonphysical realm. Rather, heaven comes to us on the earth. We will inherit a new and transformed earth, into which God will bring heaven: His rule, reign, and kingdom. Then God will conform our earthly lives, the earth itself, and the entire cosmos to heaven, His kingdom, and His presence. Or as Paul says in Romans 8:18, "the glory that is to be revealed to us!"

God always created us to be *earthly* creatures. God intended for us to relate to and commune with Him through this bodily, earthly life. Sin and death destroyed that possibility. But the Lord God restored this relationship through our earthly bodies in His incarnate Son, the Word made flesh, Jesus. As Paul says, Jesus in His resurrection is the firstfruits of the resurrected life: "But in fact Christ has been raised from the dead, the firstfruits of those who have fallen asleep" (1 Corinthians 15:20). But He is not the firstfruits only of humans, but for all of creation, which He holds in the palms of His hands, the same hands that molded the earth originally into being. Because Jesus is the firstfruits of God's glory and of our glory in God, God in and through His Son, Jesus Christ, will rule and reign on the transformed earth (the kingdom of God dwelling on earth), where He will place us to live (Revelation 22:5). Even now we hope by faith that God is preparing this glorified life in heaven and that He will bring it to realization when His Son returns in power. When we dwell in the new earth, we will see the kingdom of God all around us for we will see the face of God in the living Christ eternally.

QUESTIONS FOR DISCUSSION

What will God's kingdom on the new earth be like?

---

128   *Luther's Small Catechism with Explanation*, 20.

While the Scriptures don't provide many concrete, physical details about God's rule on earth, in Romans 14:17 Paul says it will be righteousness, joy, and peace in the Holy Spirit. The entire earth and our living on it will be filled with everything operating rightly (or righteously), everything contributing in the Spirit to the joy of everything else, and all will be at peace. There will be no conflict or division, no pain, no suffering, no evil, and no dying. All will be peaceful. One way to conceive of this is to think of what you fear the most as a threat to your life. You will not experience that fear. So, I have a mild fear of heights. I can go up into high places, but I am not daring, and I fear getting too close to the edge. On the new earth, presumably there will be heights, but I will experience no fear when walking on and approaching them.

What will it mean for the earth literally to be our home and for the city of God to come down upon the earth?

Presumably this means we will not need to worry about providing ourselves with shelter. The renewed earth and God's heavenly city will be our home, our "shelter." In Christ, however, we will need no shelter from the elements because they will no longer have the power to destroy. Could there be snow, cold temperatures, and even blizzards in the new earth? It is certainly possible. Some people find snow and blizzards beautiful. But if they are in the new earth, they will have no power to harm us. Imagine skiing through a snowstorm without experiencing any pain or cold!

Agents of the Rule and Reign of God

The promises are honestly staggering. In our new home on the renewed earth we will participate in God's rule and management of all creation. This is only possible through Jesus, who restored our human flesh to godly life through His death and resurrection. As Hebrews, quoting Psalm 8:5–6, indicates regarding Christ Jesus:

What is man, that You are mindful of him, or the son of man,
that You care for him? You made him for a little while lower than
the angels; You have crowned him with glory and honor, putting
everything in subjection under his feet. (Hebrews 2:6–8)

Through His suffering and death, the Son of God was made a little lower than the angels, but through His resurrection and ascension, God the Father has crowned Him with glory and honor and has put everything in subjection under His feet. He rules over all things.

When God resurrects us bodily on the Last Day, we, too, will participate in His rule and management over all things. The song of the saved in John's vision in Revelation proclaims the participation of the saints in the rule of God on the new earth:

> Worthy are You to take the scroll and to open its seals, for You were
> slain, and by Your blood You ransomed people for God from every
> tribe and language and people and nation, and You have made them
> a kingdom and priests to our God, and they shall reign on the earth.
> (Revelation 5:9–10)

Who is the one who opens the seals of the scroll? None other than the Paschal Lamb who was slain, Christ Jesus. Through His blood He has freed people from every language group and nation and made them a kingdom for God that will reign upon the earth. When Jesus returns, all of creation will be subject to His rule, and His adopted sons and daughters will reign on earth in His name and with His authority. We will ensure that the Word and love of God permeates the entire creation by our presence throughout the earth. As Hebrews 2:8b indicates, nothing will be left outside of Jesus' control, and so nothing will be left outside of the control of His redeemed human creatures either. Redeemed humanity will employ the Word of God in Jesus to ensure that all creation bears witness to the glory of God.

Examples of the abuse of power, authority, and control fill modern life. Husbands verbally, emotionally, physically, and sexually abuse their wives. Employers take advantage of their employees by demanding services of them that are immoral and personally humiliating. But as Jesus says to His disciples:

> It shall not be so among you. But whoever would be great among
> you must be your servant, and whoever would be first among
> you must be slave of all. For even the Son of Man came not to be
> served but to serve, and to give His life as a ransom for many.
> (Mark 10:43–45)

Jesus manifests His authority and rule in service, and so will His human creatures when they rule through Him on the earth at His return. A reign of service shows itself most clearly in love, love for all that God created, a love without any limits or boundaries. It is literally a reign of love. What Jesus commanded through His apostle John will come to full flower in the reign of God on the re-created earth:

> Beloved, let us love one another, for love is from God, and whoever loves has been born of God and knows God. Anyone who does not love does not know God, because God is love. In this the love of God was made manifest among us, that God sent His only Son into the world, so that we might live through Him. In this is love, not that we have loved God but that He loved us and sent His Son to be the propitiation for our sins. Beloved, if God so loved us, we also ought to love one another. No one has ever seen God; if we love one another, God abides in us and His love is perfected in us. (1 John 4:7–12)

The love that is from God, that we will see in the face of the risen Christ on the day of our own resurrection, is the love by which God will rule in heaven and on the earth. That love will permeate our own ruling over creation, so that we love every part of creation without exception.

Since our rule over creation is a rule of love, it is also therefore a rule that conforms to Jesus Himself and to His life among His creatures on earth. It is a rule shaped by the cross of Christ. Paul bears witness to the shape of our life, not only on this side of Christ's return, but also in the new heaven and new earth when he says:

> Have this mind among yourselves, which is yours in Christ Jesus, who, though He was in the form of God, did not count equality with God a thing to be grasped, but emptied Himself, by taking the form of a servant, being born in the likeness of men. And being found in human form, He humbled Himself by becoming obedient to the point of death, even death on a cross. Therefore God has highly exalted Him and bestowed on Him the name that is above every name, so that at the name of Jesus every knee

should bow, in heaven and on earth and under the earth, and every tongue confess that Jesus Christ is Lord, to the glory of God the Father. (Philippians 2:5–11)

When we rule over creation in Jesus, without exception we will empty ourselves in service to the needs of our fellow human creatures and the entire creation so that it may flourish and we may flourish alongside it. In other words, nature, human culture and industry, human thought and invention, the entire cultural systems and forms of humanity will be re-created and renewed to function in love as the means by which humanity lives, flourishes, and rules. Through our languages, races, cultures, cultural forms, music, art, mathematics, science, history, and memory, we will proclaim Christ as Lord and God's love in Christ forever.

QUESTIONS FOR DISCUSSION

How will the people of God rule and reign on the earth in Jesus' saving name? Will there be other people we will rule over?

Remember, this rule of God will be one of peace. When we think of ruling and governing, we think of exercising power and authority over someone or something else. But in God's eternal kingdom, the rule will be one of peace and love. We will rule over one another and all the creatures of the earth in mutual, peaceful submission. No cajoling, threats, or domination. Our wills will be one in Christ.

Had you ever before thought of heaven having languages, races, cultures, music, art, and so forth? When you think of the new heaven in that way, where does your imagination lead you?

In some way our cultures will continue to develop, but they will always be perfect at the same time. We cannot fathom continuous development that is simultaneously perfect. And the reason culture will be there is that through cultural forms, God will continue to share His great love in Christ with us. While obviously Scripture does not say every cultural form will be on the new earth, culture as the mode of earthly living will be. So, you have permission to imagine that the cultural forms that you treasure here will be there. If, like me, for instance, you can't imagine life without beer and pizza, imagine it on the renewed earth. If imagining that brings you joy, then it hits the mark because every cultural thing on the new earth will bring God's people joy.

Bodily Life in the New Heaven and the New Earth

At the end of the novella *The Great Divorce*, C. S. Lewis narrates an ongoing conversation between the primary protagonist, clearly Lewis himself, and the spirit of the dead Christian theologian George MacDonald. During this conversation with Lewis, Macdonald has a conversation with the spirit of an unbeliever who died and was sent to hell, yet has been allowed to visit heaven. The ghostly figure, who was a painter, wants there to be painting in heaven and is at a loss to find it. The conversation goes like this:

MacDonald: "When you painted on earth—at least in your earlier days—
    it was because you caught glimpses of Heaven in the earthly landscape.
    The success of your painting was that it enabled others to see the
    glimpses too. But here you are having the thing itself. It is from here
    that the messages came. There is no good telling us about this country,
    for we see it already. In fact we see it better than you do."

Ghostly Painter: "Then there's never going to be any point in painting here?"

Macdonald: "I don't say that. When you've grown into a Person (it's all
    right, we all had to do it) there'll be some things which you'll see better
    than anyone else. One of the things you'll want to do is tell us about
    them. But not yet. At present your business is to see. Come and see.
    He is endless. Come and feed."[129]

The painter wanted to contribute something of himself, his skill and art, to heaven, and without the opportunity to do so, he saw no purpose or joy in being there. Lewis's point is that heaven, or the new heaven and the new earth, is a complete gift, an endless opportunity to come and see, to come and feed. On what? On the life of God that dwells in and fills the new creation. Our cultural realities, such as painting, may find a place, but only as they help us to see the endless wonder of God's love and grace streaming through all of His transformed creation. Indeed, we will be able to feed endlessly with our eyes,

---

129   Lewis, *The Great Divorce*, 79.

ears, nose, mouth, hands, and feet upon an abundance that will never cease. Disney World can't even hold a flickering flame to what God has in store!

At the center of this endless abundance is the life of God the Father in Christ Jesus by the love of the Holy Spirit. Living in the new earth, God's redeemed creatures will be in perpetual communion at all times with the heavenly Father through His Son, Jesus Christ, in the power, love, and presence of the Holy Spirit. Literally, through the new creation itself, the means of communion with the eternal God, we will participate in the love, grace, and life of God. The life of the Trinity will permeate the entire new creation. When we eat and drink, when we laugh and sing, when we touch and embrace, when we are overwhelmed at the glory of the vistas of the new creation, when we see and interact with animals and plants of every type that God created without threat or harm, when we do all of these things, we will share in the life of the God whose Word and breath is their very life and existence. I believe that this is what Paul is trying to express when he says in 1 Corinthians 15:28, "When all things are subjected to Him, then the Son Himself will also be subjected to Him who put all things in subjection under Him, *that God may be all in all*" (emphasis added). God's life will breathe through all living things and uphold every element of creation. It is this for which we, who must still physically die, long. As the Eastern theologian Alexander Schmemann says:

> Although death is conquered and transformed, abolished as separation from God and thus from life, even made into blessedness—it is *not* the ultimate fulfillment. It is still "a way": the way to the resurrection, to the final victory of God, to the new heaven and earth, to the fulfillment of the kingdom of God when God shall be "all in all." For this ultimate victory the Church waits. This waiting is the content of her very life, the victory anticipated by her members, whether alive or dead.[130]

We long not just to conquer death but to live forever in communion with the Source of life, to live in perpetual relationship with the One who is life itself: Father, Son, and Holy Spirit. In the new creation, no longer are human beings in love with the world for themselves. Rather they are in love with God through the world for the sake of their fellow human beings and the world. A

---

130   Alexander Schmemann, *The Liturgy of Death*, 97–98.

human does not love the kingdom of God for the sake of painting. Rather, a human being loves the kingdom of God and God present in it, and so receives painting through which God's kingdom, love, and presence are experienced and revealed. This experience of God's life and love is, Peter says, the "inheritance that is imperishable, undefiled, and unfading, kept in heaven for you" (1 Peter 1:4).

In the midst of Jesus' Sermon on the Mount, teaching on the kingdom of God, He says:

> Do not lay up for yourselves treasures on earth, where moth and rust destroy and where thieves break in and steal, but lay up for yourselves treasures in heaven, where neither moth nor rust destroys and where thieves do not break in and steal. For where your treasure is, there your heart will be also. (Matthew 6:19–21)

Where do you find your treasure? Clearly, in heaven. But what kind of treasure is Jesus talking about here? He's not speaking about streets of gold or diamond-studded gates and houses. We cannot find that treasure on this death-permeated earth. At the end of this life, that is all there is—death. That is all there is in this earthly life: communion with *death*. So where do you find your treasure? Where your heart is. And in your heart, the seat of your being, life, and faith, God's treasure has found you—in the One who is victor over death, who is in communion with the life of God, His Father, who is Himself the Living One. The Son of Man, Jesus, the Christ, has found you! In Him is life, the only life, your only true life. It has found you. That is where your treasure is, where Jesus is and will be on the final day, revealing His peace and love to the entire creation.[131]

The treasure of heaven is to live in the streams of God's life, where there cannot be and never will be death. It is the fulfillment of the promise Jesus gave to the woman at the well: "The water that I will give him will become in him a spring of water welling up to eternal life" (John 4:14). Living an eternal life means being in communion with the One who is eternal and who shares an eternal life with one another: Father, Son, and Holy Spirit. In heaven on earth

---

131 In his book *O Death, Where Is Thy Sting?*, 59, Alexander Schmemann, quoting another Eastern Orthodox theologian, Sergius Bulgakov, indicates that in the Paschal Feast, the Easter Vigil, and Easter Sunday worship, the Christian receives a foretaste of the feast of God, of this treasure.

we will be united to the eternal life of Father, Son, and Holy Spirit, as Jesus promises in John 17:20–21: "I do not ask for these only, but also for those who will believe in Me through their word, that they may all be one, just as You, Father, are in Me, and I in You, that they also may be in Us, so that the world may believe that You have sent Me." We will live and move and have our being in the triune God, in eternal communion with God. C. S. Lewis describes it this way in The Great Divorce: "'What needs could I have,' she said, 'now that I have all? I am full now, not empty. I am *In Love Himself* [italics added], not lonely. Strong, not weak. You shall be the same. Come and see.'"[132] To be "In Love Himself" is to be in Christ—a mystery we cannot fully fathom now—and through Him to share the life of His Father and the Spirit of life and love.

In our bodily life on the new earth we will dwell with and see God through the Son of God, Jesus, our Lord. This is the nature of Jesus' promise to those who believe in Him:

> Let not your hearts be troubled. Believe in God; believe also
> in Me. In My Father's house are many rooms. If it were not so,
> would I have told you that I go to prepare a place for you? And if I
> go and prepare a place for you, I will come again and will take you
> to Myself, that where I am you may be also. (John 14:1–3)

Where Jesus is, which will be in His kingdom ("My Father's house") that has come down to the transformed earth, that is where we will be. We will see God in Christ personally, dwell in His light that never fades (Revelation 21:23), and live on the earth where God has located His temple, His divine dwelling (v. 22). By seeing God through Christ with our own glorified eyes and bodies, we will reflect God's light and glory. We will fully reveal in our bodies the image of God (Matthew 13:43). C. S. Lewis describes the love and glory we will radiate as coming from all our limbs, as though that love and glory were some liquid in which we had bathed.[133]

At the center of communion with the triune God in heaven on earth is Christ, the one who still is and eternally will be God and humanity united in one. He is at the center of our living in relationship with the Father and

---

132   Lewis, *The Great Divorce*, 111.

133   Ibid., 107.

the Spirit who cannot be seen. Even after God establishes His rule and reign following the Day of Judgment, God the Father continues to mediate life to us through the Word made flesh, crucified and raised for us. Everything we will do—breathing, thinking, loving (to name a few)—we will do in Christ. God will transform our lives in Christ and through Christ. The water of life and the tree of life that John describes in Revelation 22 will feed us, and that river and that tree, of course, are Jesus:

> Then the angel showed me the river of the water of life, bright as crystal, flowing from the throne of God and of the Lamb through the middle of the street of the city; also, on either side of the river, the tree of life with its twelve kinds of fruit, yielding its fruit each month. The leaves of the tree were for the healing of the nations. (Revelation 22:1–2)

John is revealing what is already true: even now our lives are hidden with Christ (Colossians 3:3), and John sees those same but transformed lives revealed in the new heaven and new earth. God will transform our lives to conform them to His Son, Jesus Christ. We will be recognizable as the humans God created us to be, but in our bodies and our actions we will become and be the image of Christ. As John says, "Beloved, we are God's children now, and what we will be has not yet appeared; but we know that when He appears we shall be like Him, because we shall see Him as He is" (1 John 3:2). In his *Chronicles of Narnia*, C. S. Lewis describes the transformation of Eustace in the third volume, *The Voyage of the Dawn Treader*. Eustace is a greedy, unlikable child whom the Pevensie children have met. He falls asleep atop the treasure trove of a dying dragon (where your treasure is, there will your heart be also!). When he awakes, he has been transformed into a dragon, scales, tail, and all, reflecting his inner character and desires. Only Aslan, the Christ figure, can transform him by stripping off with his claws Eustace's dragon skin down to his raw human skin. Upon bathing him, Aslan dresses him in new clothes (an image of Baptism[134]). It is a radical, deadly transformation. Yet, that is the transformation that will happen to all who were washed in Christ in the water of Baptism, when their bodies are raised on the Last Day. We will see ourselves clothed in Christ alone.

---

134   I am indebted to J. Richard Middleton, *A New Heaven and a New Earth*, 209, for these insights into C. S. Lewis.

QUESTIONS FOR DISCUSSION

When you think of the abundance of the new heaven and earth, what do you imagine? How would you describe your ideal of the new heaven and earth? How does it compare with God's vision?

> Our imagination can paint a new heaven and new earth that is an ideal. We imagine it shaped by the primary things that capture our desires and interests in this life. But that is too limiting a vision. It would be more accurate to describe it as an endless opportunity to come and see God's life and God's creation.

Where is your treasure located? Are your treasures in heaven?

> By this question, Jesus is asking us where our trust and ultimate desires lie. Are your trust and desire located on earth with earthly things like money, family, politics, sports, games, human relationships, and so forth? Our treasure should be focused where Jesus is, in heaven, preparing the new earth and the new heaven. That should be where we focus our trust and desires. That is the place from which eternal life will come.

What does it mean to you to be conformed to Christ when God raises your body on the Last Day?

> It doesn't mean that we will look like Christ or be some mirror image of Christ. We will have our own bodies that will in some way be in continuity with the bodies we have now. But Jesus will recognizably fill who we are and how we live. The virtues of the Spirit, which Jesus Himself embodies, will permeate our bodies and our lives.

A Spiritual Body

To be clothed in Christ is a powerful image. Paul indicates that the people of God "wait eagerly for adoption as sons, *the redemption of our bodies*" (Romans 8:23; emphasis added). So what does the redemption of our bodies look like? As we already saw in chapter 4, Paul proclaims the hope of the resurrection:

> So is it with the resurrection of the dead. What is sown is perishable; what is raised is imperishable. It is sown in dishonor; it is raised in

glory. It is sown in weakness; it is raised in power. It is sown a natural body; it is raised a spiritual body. If there is a natural body, there is also a spiritual body. Thus it is written, "The first man Adam became a living being"; the last Adam became a life-giving spirit. (1 Corinthians 15:42–45)

God will raise our bodies as spiritual bodies, for it is in Jesus, the life-giving spirit, that God resurrects us and glorifies us. Paul clearly expresses that this entails the glorifying of our bodies: "But our citizenship is in heaven, and from it we await a Savior, the Lord Jesus Christ, who will transform our lowly body to be like His glorious body, by the power that enables Him even to subject all things to Himself" (Philippians 3:20–21). Christ will renew our bodies so that spiritually they become like His body, transformed and glorified.

We don't know exactly what our spiritual bodies will look like. Only the truly spiritual can know this, and we have not fully become spiritual, physical creatures yet (see 1 Corinthians 2:14). Yet, the Word of God does enable us to give a very elemental description of our glorified existence in the new heaven and the new earth. We know that there will be both discontinuity and continuity between our preresurrection earthly bodies and our spiritual bodies on the day of resurrection. The old body must die and be transformed. It will not be exactly the same as the body God gave you when you were conceived.[135] Your raised body will not be the same as the body you inherited from your father Adam. But there will also be continuity! As Paul says in 1 Corinthians 15:53, "For this perishable body must put on the imperishable, and this mortal body must put on immortality." This perishable body, the body inherited from Adam, which God created, will put on the imperishable, the body of the Second Adam, Jesus Christ. The imperishable body will in some way be the transformed body that is currently wasting away. Changing skins or bodies is like changing clothes. Your new body will be a new form of clothing, but it will still be human clothing or flesh, not dinosaur skin, and will, in some way, be the transformed flesh and blood with which we lived in this earthly life.

---

135   See 1 Corinthians 15:35–38. Paul says that the body that is sown into the ground in death is not the body that will be. At first Mary Magdalene and the disciples did not recognize Jesus when they encountered Him after His resurrection, but when they heard His voice and saw His wounds, they knew that it was the Lord. (See John 20.) The same presumably will be true of our resurrected bodies.

QUESTIONS FOR DISCUSSION

When you think of having a glorified physical body, where does your imagination lead you? What do you think that glorified body will be like?

> The spirit and the body are not at odds with each other. God created them both and gave us both body and spirit. Thus, to have a glorified body in a sense means to have a perfected version of our current composition as creatures. But there will be a full integration between body and spirit. They will be even more substantive and solid than they are in our current earthly life, filled with the solidity and permanence of God's eternal kingdom. And they will shine and radiate the goodness and glory of God.

If God gave you the option to choose what was in continuity and what was in discontinuity between your current earthly body and the glorified body of the new heaven and earth, what would you choose to be in continuity and what would you leave behind?

> Personally, I'd leave behind my balding head and my poorly constructed nasal passages (a really poor sense of smell) and keep the bushy eyebrows, the wavy hair, and my general appearance. But even more important, I'd leave behind my lack of timeliness, the occasional lack of assertiveness, and my self-righteousness. Ultimately we want enough of ourselves that within the glory of Christ, others will know it's us—but "us" with all our sins, weaknesses, and personal inadequacies left behind.

Spiritual: God's Life Reflected in Our Bodies

Let's explore the two aspects of our resurrected bodies, spiritual and physical, and what we can say about both while still seeing through a glass darkly. In both spiritual and physical characteristics after the resurrection, the nature of our body will always reflect the fact that it is forever in communion with God in Christ. That means we can never possess anything that is contrary to God's being and life, and that everything we do possess will reflect our communion with God. Our bodies will reflect communion with Life with a capital *L*, the only life that truly *is* Life, the Life of the Father, Son, and Holy Spirit. To be living in and from the Life of God is to have a spiritual body.

Our spiritual bodies will reflect the life of God. Expressed in terms of both what is absent and what is present, we can describe our spiritual bodies in the following way. As Job declares (19:26–27) and as Paul confirms (1 Corinthians 13:12), we will personally, in our bodies, see God in Christ. God will give us the opportunity to see and know God through our relationship to Christ Jesus as God truly is. While we cannot fully know God as God knows God, we will, within the capacities of our human intellect, will, and body, know God as God is. We will see God face to face in the Son of God, Jesus, and know God as all truth, goodness, and love. This face-to-face knowledge of God will be the source of eternal joy and happiness. C. S. Lewis puts it this way: You will be able to *taste* the truth of God just like you taste honey.[136]

This beautiful and joyous vision of God's face is the source of many other beautiful characteristics of our living as spiritual bodies. By the power of the Holy Spirit that will spiritually fill the entirety of our beings, God will dwell in us, and so will the fullness of God's unrelenting love. We will live within and be surrounded by the love of God constantly. Being filled with such love includes the absence of sin, evil, struggle, suffering, sorrow (Isaiah 25:8), and death (Romans 7:24). As John sees in his great apocalyptic revelation, "He will wipe away every tear from their eyes, and death shall be no more, neither shall there be mourning, nor crying, nor pain anymore, for the former things have passed away" (Revelation 21:4). Whatever evil, sin, and suffering we can conceive of now—child abuse, sexual abuse, murder—will be inconceivable in the vision of the Father through His Son in the presence of His Spirit. The absence of evil means that we will live in perfect joy and happiness in the presence of God. Through this complete joy God will give us complete rest and peace. Nothing will trouble His creatures or anything in His new heaven and new earth. We will enter the rest and peace that is God's life (Hebrews 4:1–6).

In the transformed earth, God will give His creatures bodies that will not perish or die (immortal). Our bodies will never grow weak, but always will be filled with strength, glory, and beauty that is appropriate for those filled with the Life of God. Thus Paul writes, "So is it with the resurrection of the

---

136   Lewis, *The Great Divorce*, 44.

dead. What is sown is perishable; what is raised is imperishable. It is sown in dishonor; it is raised in glory. It is sown in weakness; it is raised in power" (1 Corinthians 15:42–43). So we will live in the eternity of God's Life. Our life in the new heaven and the new earth will be timeless, not bound by time or a beginning and an end. But it will be even more than that. We will not even be conscious of time or conceive of our lives from the framework of time, because we will simply live in the Father, Son, and Holy Spirit, who are life without limit. Life unbound by time is life in its completeness and fullness, the Life of God.

QUESTION FOR DISCUSSION

Which of the realities of our spiritual life in the new earth captivates you most fully?

> For me it is eternal joy and the absence of all evil. For you it may be the absence of suffering and sickness, the knowledge of all truth, or something else. All of this finally reflects the Father, Son, and Holy Spirit as the source of life and all things good according to God's will.

Image God on the New Earth

Our relationship with Father, Son, and Holy Spirit through the resurrection of Jesus and the restoration of God's image in us through Him is the basis for the glorification of our bodies. In the new creation we still will relate to one another and to the whole new creation through our risen physical bodies. Only on this new earth will we relate to one another through glorified bodies that perfectly reflect the love and wisdom of God. Both the spiritual and physical realities of our glorified bodies are united as we see the face of God. So, in the new creation we will reflect fully the image of the triune God throughout the new heaven, earth, and all creation. God's divine presence will permeate all of heaven and earth, the entire transformed cosmos. We also as God's people will reflect His image and presence throughout all the earth. Paul indicates that Jesus ascended "far above all the heavens, that He might fill all things" (Ephesians 4:10). The rule and reign of God will fill all of the new creation. Those who image God, whose bodies God has transformed through death and resurrection and made bodies of the Spirit, will bear witness that heaven has come down to earth in the presence of Jesus Christ. The saints will dwell in this glorious land bearing witness to God's abundant life.

QUESTION FOR DISCUSSION

Have you ever thought about what you might be doing in our earthly paradise? Again, where does your imagination lead you?

> As we noted before, we may be doing many of the things we did on this earth, but perfectly and without the loss of energy or any experience of suffering. While we can't be specific about what we may be doing in building the culture of the resurrected earth, we do know we will share in together imaging God to all creation. We will be the vehicles who will fill every corner and location on God's new earth with His image, light, and truth.

Physical: Relating to One Another and the New Earth through Our Bodies in the New Creation

Just as God calls human beings to fulfill certain responsibilities (such as extending the human race, ruling over and subduing an unruly creation, insuring justice among people and for the sake of the creation, and so forth) as His agents in the fallen creation, God will continue to call His creatures to fulfill certain responsibilities and callings in the new creation. When we are spiritual persons, these callings will be completely transformed. We will carry them out in effortless ways. Everything we do will be filled with love for God and love for our neighbor. We will rejoice to see the creation flourish, and we will do so without regret or anguish for the ways in which we gave of ourselves that it might flourish. In the giving of ourselves and in the new creation's giving to us, nothing will suffer, perish, die, or be lost. For example, as we water the new creation, not a single drop of water will be wasted or lost. And yet every plant, animal, and person will drink what it needs to live in beauty and strength. Even in our loving self-giving to others, everything will remain complete and whole within God's eternal life.

The entire new creation will be substantively real, even more substantive than the current creation unmoored from the bedrock of God's living Word.

In the new creation, the Word, the living Lord, will be the bedrock and foundation that upholds all reality. In *The Great Divorce*, C. S. Lewis says that "Heaven is reality itself. All that is fully real is Heavenly. For all that can be shaken will be shaken and only the unshakable remains."[137] For this reason Lewis conveys a heavenly earth that is more physical and substantive than our current planet. Those who are in the heavenly earth are *solid* people, unlike the unsubstantial ghosts or waifs who are in hell. Lewis describes the physical substance of the new earth through his main character (presumably Lewis himself) in this way:

> I saddled away on some vague pretext, of doing a little exploring. A grove of huge cedars to my right seemed attractive and I entered it. Walking proved difficult. The grass, hard as diamonds to my unsubstantial feet, made me feel as if I were walking on wrinkled rock, and I suffered pains like those of the mermaid in Hans Andersen. A bird ran across in front of me and I envied it. It belonged to that country [the new earth] and was as real as the grass. It could bend the stalks and spatter itself with the dew.[138]

In this new creation, light will permeate everything, filling the whole creation with a lustrous and shining appearance. Clearly Lewis's vision of the new creation develops out of the apostle John's apocalyptic vision:

> Then the angel showed me the river of the water of life, bright as crystal, flowing from the throne of God and of the Lamb through the middle of the street of the city; also, on either side of the river, the tree of life with its twelve kinds of fruit, yielding its fruit each month. The leaves of the tree were for the healing of the nations. No longer will there be anything accursed, but the throne of God and of the Lamb will be in it, and His servants will worship Him. They will see His face, and His name will be on their foreheads. And night will be no more. They will need no light of lamp or sun, for the Lord God will be their light, and they will reign forever and ever. (Revelation 22:1–5)

---

137   Ibid., 68. See also Hebrews 11:10.

138   Lewis, *The Great Divorce*, 32.

As the redeemed, raised to dwell with Christ forever, we live in our bodies in the solid and never-fading new creation of God.

In that new creation will be the most glorious family reunion imaginable. It will be a reunion of those washed in the blood of the Lamb from all languages and peoples. They will gather around the unending heavenly feast that God is preparing. We can expect to feast with all those whom we loved on the old earth who by faith participated in God's salvation in Christ. And we'll also do so with those whom we didn't love as fully as we should have. What we experience in the Lord's Supper will reach its endless consummation on the new earth, as Isaiah describes it: "On this mountain the LORD of hosts will make for all peoples a feast of rich food, a feast of well-aged wine, of rich food full of marrow, of aged wine well refined" (Isaiah 25:6). In that feast we will see those who shine more radiantly than even we perceive ourselves. For their glory will bear witness to their earthly lives filled with faith, hope, and love. And there will be no jealousy or regret in their greater glory than ours. We will be united in love, and through that love we will share in their glory through the love of God in the most glorified one, our Lord Jesus.[139]

All who are united in love in that renewed creation will rejoice together to glorify God through our living in the new heaven and feasting with one another on the abundance of God's life. As Augustine, the great fifth-century Church Father, said, "There we shall be still and see; we shall see and we shall love; we shall love and we shall praise. Behold what will be in the end, without end! For what is our end but to reach the kingdom which has no end?"[140] Endless praise filling the new creation seems the only logical response to what God will do:

> Then I saw a new heaven and a new earth, for the first heaven and the first earth had passed away, and the sea was no more. And I saw the holy city, new Jerusalem, coming down out of heaven from God, prepared as a bride adorned for her husband. And I heard a loud voice from the throne saying, "Behold, the dwelling place of God is with man. He will dwell with them, and they will be His people, and God Himself will be with them as their God. He will

---

139   For biblical references to distinctions of glory in the new earth, see 1 Corinthians 3:8; 15:40–41; 2 Corinthians 9:6.

140   Augustine, *City of God*, 22.30; *MPL* 41:804.5.

wipe away every tear from their eyes, and death shall be no more, neither shall there be mourning, nor crying, nor pain anymore, for the former things have passed away. (Revelation 21:1–4)

QUESTIONS FOR DISCUSSION

The apostle John's vision of the new heaven and earth in Revelation 22 is evocative. How would you describe it to someone else?

There is no right answer here. But your description to someone else should reflect the substance of the new earth (living water, healing fruit, the all-permeating light of God) and God's presence at the center.

How does a great family reunion strike you as an image for paradise? What does it help you to understand about the Church on earth and the kingdom of God in the new heaven and earth?

God's family reunion in Jesus is not based on nationality or ethnicity or tribe or skin color. It is based on adoption into God's family by faith through Baptism into Jesus. Family reunions here on earth can create an expansive vision, because we probably all have relatives that we would prefer not be at the table. In the heavenly kingdom all such reservations will be left behind and we will rejoice to sit at table with all our brothers and sisters of whatever stripe and background.

Have you ever thought about distinctions in glory in the new heaven and new earth?

These distinctions in glory do not mean that the triune God is any less accessible to any of the saints. But think of it this way: I expect to see Peter and Paul shining in ways that draw us more closely to Christ, shining even more gloriously than I will. And I expect to say the same thing of my sainted grandfather because of his life of faith on earth. I want them all to receive such honor!

Conclusion

For now, life in God's heavenly creation waits. We live in this life, which culminates in death, filled with hope for what is to come. We live now into the future, and the vision of life in the rule and reign of God in God's Word surrounds our hope. Alexander Schmemann describes what we hope for in this way:

> It is not simply a belief that somewhere, at some point beyond the confines of this life, our existence will continue—this idea existed even before Christ. But in the fact that the world itself and life itself have once more received purpose and meaning, that time itself has become filled with light, that eternity has entered into our life already here and now. Eternity is first of all the knowledge of God, which is open to us through Christ. There is no more loneliness, there is no more fear and darkness. I am with you, says Christ, I am with you now and always, with complete love, with all knowledge, with all power. Eternity is the commandment of love that Christ left us. "By this all men will know that you are my disciples, if you have love for one another" (John 13:35). And finally the name of this eternity is "peace and joy in the Holy Spirit" (Romans 14:17), and of this joy Christ says, "no one will take your joy from you" (John 16:22). Salvation is nothing less than all of this.[141]

All of this is heaven on earth, our salvation in the new heaven and the new earth. For now, as Paul says, "We see in a mirror dimly, but then face to face. Now I know in part; then I shall know fully, even as I have been fully known" (1 Corinthians 13:12). We will see God and one another face to face, fully and completely as we live as God's children. And we shall know God even as God knows us fully and completely, nothing hidden, nothing shameful before His all-seeing eye. Come, Lord Jesus. Come quickly.

---

141   Schmemann, *O Death, Where Is Thy Sting?*, 86–87.

Jerusalem, My Happy Home

1. Jerusalem, my happy home,
   When shall I come to thee?
   When shall my sorrows have an end?
   Thy joys when shall I see?

2. O happy harbor of the saints,
   O sweet and pleasant soil!
   In thee no sorrow may be found,
   No grief, no care, no toil.

3. Thy gardens and thy gallant walks
   Continually are green;
   There grow such sweet and pleasant flow'rs
   As nowhere else are seen.

4. There trees forevermore bear fruit
   And evermore do spring;
   There evermore the angels dwell
   And evermore do sing.

5. Apostles, martyrs, prophets, there
   Around my Savior stand;
   And soon my friends in Christ below
   Will join the glorious band.

6. O Christ, do Thou my soul prepare
   For that bright home of love
   That I may see Thee and adore
   With all Thy saints above.

Text: F. B. P., 16th cent., alt. Public domain.

COMFORTING HYMNS
AND CHRISTIAN SONGS

Hymns and Christian songs are a great way to bring joy and peace to those who are walking through the shadow of death. The Psalms have always been a comforting place to rest when struggling with grief, death, and the unknown. But hymns and Christian music can also bring comfort especially when you are planning a funeral service or struggling with the grief that follows. This section is not just for pastors, choral directors, or others who are preparing a funeral service but is meant to provide comfort to all who are grieving the loss of family and friends. If you are nearing death or grieving the death of a loved one, these hymns and songs will bring great comfort and hope because they help you fix your eyes on Jesus, His resurrection, the new creation, and the resurrected body that all believers will have throughout eternity. This is Christ's promise to us.

There are so many hymns and songs to choose from, but these were chosen specifically because their text highlights the joy the Christian has because of Christ's resurrection promise. They bring comfort not only to those who have lost a loved one, but to those who are in the midst of dying. They can bring comfort in the days before and in the days that follow a death and even at the burial site itself as they help us turn our focus from the death we are experiencing with our eyes to the joy our loved one is now experiencing in paradise, and the glorious resurrection that is to come.

When Peace, like a River

Many are the afflictions of the righteous, but the
LORD delivers him out of them all. (Psalm 34:19)

"When Peace, like a River" expresses Horatio G. Spafford's deep and great loss between the years of 1871, when his four-year-old son died suddenly of scarlet fever, and 1873, when he lost his four daughters in a tragic shipwreck.

His wife survived the shipwreck, but was found unconscious clinging to a piece of the wreckage. Days after the wreck, on his way to join his wife, near the place the ship went down and restless from lack of sleep, he said, "It is well; the will of God be done."

His hymn brings comfort by looking to Christ's pain, His affliction on the cross. In the final stanza the text turns to the promised day of Christ's return when He will raise our bodies and live with us forever in the new creation.

I Can Only Imagine

> Behold, I am making a covenant. Before all your people I will do marvels, such as have not been created in all the earth or in any nation. And all the people among whom you are shall see the work of the LORD, for it is an awesome thing that I will do with you. (Exodus 34:10)

"I Can Only Imagine" was written by Bart Millard after the death of his father to express his love and forgiveness for the man who had abused him his entire life. As Bart would say, "If God can change a wretched heart like my father's and forgive him, so can I."

This music asks what it might be like to see Jesus face to face following death: Will I be so deeply in awe I will not be able to speak? Will I dance? Will I bow down and worship?

Abide with Me

> If you abide in Me, and My words abide in you, ask whatever you desire, and it will be done for you. (John 15:7)

This piece, which probably started as a poem, was written by Henry Francis Lyte, a pastor serving a fishing village in England. Henry struggled with a lung condition and was diagnosed with tuberculosis while in his fifties. To help slow the tuberculosis, he planned a therapeutic holiday in Italy. The day before leaving he shared a copy of his poem "Abide with Me." Henry died that same year while in Italy after sending a revised version of the poem home to his wife.

Throughout this hymn, Henry pleads with God to be near him, to never leave him, to abide with him now as He has his entire life. Although Henry sees and feels the darkness of death pressing in on him, he clings to the promise of Christ and His unfailing presence.

Amazing Grace

> In Him we have redemption through His blood, the forgiveness of our trespasses, according to the riches of His grace.
> (Ephesians 1:7)

"Amazing Grace" was written by John Newton, whose mother died when John was only seven. After her death John's life drifted away, literally out to sea, as he served in the British Navy. One day he deserted, but was quickly captured and flogged for his behavior. His life had become such a mess that he daily vacillated between thoughts of murder and suicide.

In March 1748, he and the rest of the crew were literally jolted awake by a brutal storm that would change his life forever. John became one of the most powerful evangelical preachers of his time in Britain and the author of literally hundreds of hymns.

This hymn is all about God's amazing grace. When we are overwhelmed by times of sadness or sorrow, it turns our focus to Jesus' suffering, reminding us of all He did for us.

Jesus, Remember Me

> Jesus, remember me when You come into Your kingdom.
> (Luke 23:42)

Jacques Berthier wrote this simple lyric and tune in 1978. His idea was to focus on a few lines of Scripture or liturgy in a repetitive fashion to allow for meditation on the words themselves.

The text of this piece gives us the opportunity to pour ourselves upon Christ, as we plead for Him to remember. It seems to have been written from the perspective of a poor beggar, the thief on the cross, who much like ourselves had nothing to offer. We likewise plead with Jesus to remember us when He comes into His kingdom.

Love Divine, All Loves Excelling

> Therefore, if anyone is in Christ, he is a new creation.
> The old has passed away; behold, the new has come.
> (2 Corinthians 5:17)

Charles Wesley addressed this hymn to Christ. It begins as a prayer asking Jesus to dwell within us so that He might humble us and fill us with compassion in order to serve all we meet.

Stanza 3 turns our thoughts to the way we receive our everlasting life in Christ. It cries to Christ to return and never leave again, for His second coming. Stanza 4 asks Him to finish His new creation. In a time of loss or mourning one might turn to this hymn to remind us that all God's children will dwell together in the new heavens and new earth and reside with Christ forever.

No Saint on Earth Lives Life to Self Alone

> For I am sure that neither death nor life, nor angels nor rulers,
> nor things present nor things to come, nor powers, nor height
> nor depth, nor anything else in all creation, will be able to
> separate us from the love of God in Christ Jesus our Lord.
> (Romans 8:38–39)

Little is known about this hymn and its author, J. W. Schulte-Nordholt. But the text of the hymn speak mountains of God's amazing love for His children. Nothing at all can separate us from the love of our Creator, except if we turn our back on Him. The text is only two lines packed with promise, hope, love, truth, and life.

Be Still, My Soul

> Be still, and know that I am God. I will be exalted
> among the nations, I will be exalted in the earth!
> (Psalm 46:10)

Catharina Amalia Dorothea von Schlegel lived for a hundred years (1697–1797), quite a feat at that time. She lived in a Protestant nunnery at an Evangelical Lutheran endowment in Germany. Her hymn text can be our prayer when our hearts are so filled with sorrow or grief that our thoughts can't form the words. It's a prayer pulled from deep inside, a reminder that we can always wait on God because He will faithfully be there in the future as He has in the past.

Lord, It Belongs Not to My Care

Nevertheless, not My will, but Yours, be done.
(Luke 22:42)

Richard Baxter wrote the hymn "Lord, It Belongs Not to My Care" in the 1600s. After taking his Holy Orders, he served as the Curate of Kidderminster a good portion of his life. Today this is best understood as one who preaches. He is known for his work in prose and poetry.

The hymn's message is to trust in the Lord no matter life's circumstances. The text leads the reader through the dark days of life, but also recognizes that they will never be as dark as the days Christ walked on the way to the cross.

God's Own Child, I Gladly Say It (stanza 4)

Do you not know that all of us who were baptized into
Christ Jesus were baptized into His death? We were
buried therefore with Him by baptism into death, in
order that, just as Christ was raised from the dead by the
glory of the Father, we too might walk in newness of life.
(Romans 6:3–4)

Erdmann Neumeister (1671–1756) was a schoolmaster, organist, and pastor. This hymn proclaims over and over, "I am baptized into Christ." It reminds us that in Christ our life, our death, our everything, is secured. Death may claim me physically, but Christ has claimed me eternally. At my death I am a child of paradise.

Lord, Thee I Love with All My Heart

> We do not want you to be uninformed, brothers, about
> those who are asleep, that you may not grieve as others
> do who have no hope. . . . So we will always be with the
> Lord. Therefore encourage one another with these words.
> (1 Thessalonians 4:13, 17–18)

This three-stanza hymn was written by Martin Schalling, a favorite pupil of Philip Melanchthon, who cowrote the Book of Concord with Martin Luther. The first two stanzas help the reader focus on loving, trusting, and depending on God alone. Then, because of Christ's sacrifice for us, we are able to love and serve our neighbor. At the end of stanza 2, the text turns us to our own death and the comfort we find in trusting Christ's sacrifice. Stanza 3 brings it all home. In death, we pray God to send His angels to guide us to the presence of Christ and to those who have gone before us. We ask Him to keep our bodies until Christ reappears and awakens them from sleep that we may walk in glory with Christ forever.

When we become fearful or uncertain about death, this hymn offers the blessed assurance of not only our resurrected bodies but life with Christ forever. His love and His promise will be our guide, and Christ's words of promise will be fulfilled.

This Joyful Eastertide

> If Christ has not been raised, then our preaching is in vain
> and your faith is in vain. . . . But in fact Christ has been raised
> from the dead, the firstfruits of those who have fallen asleep.
> (1 Corinthians 15:14, 20)

You can't very well provide a list of hymns as resources without including an Easter hymn. George Ratcliffe Woodward expresses the confidence and joy every Christian has because Christ has been raised from the dead. Woodward was an ordained pastor of the Church of England.

"This Joyful Eastertide" promises that our faith is *not* in vain because Jesus *was* raised from the dead. Death will claim us temporarily but cannot hold us because Christ Himself has conquered sin and death and He was bodily raised from the dead. So, when it looks to the rest of the world as if death has won, we know without a doubt that Christ won and gives us the victory.

Psalm 77

Psalm 77 is a wonderful reminder of what we all need to hear when we are struggling through life's tough days. Many believers turn away from their faith or at least drift away for a while after the death of a loved one. We need to be angry with someone; we need to blame all this pain and sorrow on someone. What are we to do? Where can we go to relieve the pain we are feeling?

Cry or pray the words of Psalm 77 and you will discover He has always been and will always be there. These words assure you that God has always been right there beside you:

> I cry aloud to God, aloud to God, and He will hear me.
> In the day of my trouble I seek the Lord; in the night my
> hand is stretched out without wearying; my soul refuses
> to be comforted. When I remember God, I moan; when
> I meditate, my spirit faints.

> You hold my eyelids open; I am so troubled that I cannot speak.
> I consider the days of old, the years long ago. I said, "Let me
> remember my song in the night; let me meditate in my heart."
> Then my spirit made a diligent search: "Will the Lord spurn
> forever, and never again be favorable? Has His steadfast love
> forever ceased? Are His promises at an end for all time? Has
> God forgotten to be gracious? Has He in anger shut up His
> compassion?"

> Then I said, "I will appeal to this, to the years of the right hand
> of the Most High."

> I will remember the deeds of the LORD; yes, I will remember
> Your wonders of old. I will ponder all Your work, and meditate
> on Your mighty deeds. Your way, O God, is holy. What god is
> great like our God? You are the God who works wonders; You
> have made known Your might among the peoples.

You with Your arm redeemed Your people, the children of Jacob and Joseph.

When the waters saw you, O God, when the waters saw You, they were afraid; indeed, the deep trembled. The clouds poured out water; the skies gave forth thunder; Your arrows flashed on every side. The crash of Your thunder was in the whirlwind; Your lightnings lighted up the world; the earth trembled and shook. Your way was through the sea, Your path through the great waters; yet Your footprints were unseen. You led Your people like a flock by the hand of Moses and Aaron.